Jobs Will Happen

Edward J. Morawski

ISBN 978-0-557-48803-2

Dedicated to all those people seeking jobs

Contents

Chapter 1

What is The Big Picture?

The "Big Picture" is that vision or image of how things work that all people carry around with them and use to evaluate their position in life. Even when people deny it their behavior reveals the perception that guides every action or retreat they seek. When it comes to work and the jobs people do this "Big Picture" concept is a driving force behind each person's daily pursuit and how they make their way in life. Although the image of the world may drive initial behavior it is the repetition of acts that keep a person in a path that has little variation. The examples of this are numerous for all of us.

Is your view of the world somewhere within the following examples? Take the unemployed auto worker as an example, since they are so numerous today. Life in an auto company over the last 20 years or so, was generally a good life that required being there and staying within the bounds of good behavior if you expected to gain stature in the community regardless of being either in a union or on the salary side of the aisle. Much is said about the abuse of rules that protect either hourly or salary workers, but the calamity of the industry was brought to a head by an outside world that changed the customer buying habits in days not years. The individual auto worker then encountered a "Big Picture" that did not agree with much of what most had understood as a way to make their way in life up to that time.

All the behavior that was so practiced on a daily basis no longer applied to the new realities of everyday life. The transition from an old world view to a new world view will take years, just as it did for farmers and their families or steel workers and their families. Even the most enterprising of individuals were met with a marketplace that needed less of everything with housing and automobiles at the top of the list. Who among the many were rewarded with a steady stream of income? People that had established multiple sources of income and options for alternative jobs ahead of the collapse of the marketplace were among the survivors that are part of the new job force going forward. Who among those that have lost greatly will regain their stature in an economy with rules that have not been written by any union, company or government agency? You can be among the many if you choose to be through small everyday decisions that will guide your action for some time to come.

Another segment of the job market that has been greatly impacted is the home industry. If you built homes, sold homes, supplied accessories or materials for homes or had anything to do with banking or investment you have been impacted. Like the auto industry some of this was looked at as cyclical, but the enormous number of foreclosures drove a collapse in banking and investment unseen for decades. When national unemployment rises above ten percent generally everybody knows someone or many that are grappling with job dislocation. Who will be part of a more prosperous tomorrow that has yet to be established? You can be among the many if you choose to be through small everyday decisions that establish new habits that are rewarded by a marketplace that is unlike what generally existed up until a year ago.

Automobiles, homes, banking and investment are not inclusive of all those people impacted but are instead inclusive of those people that have had to seriously rethink their approach to how they make their way in the world or in other words rethink the "Big Picture". For some it has been devastating and has cost them all they own, for others the impact has been severe, but has yet to be realized and for a minority it has solidified their new world view that will guide them to prosperity in the future. Maybe it is too much to expect prosperity for all people, but hope for all people that take advantage of limited opportunity to rework their behavior in a way that recognizes the reality around them is not too great an expectation. History is full of examples of people that overcame failure and disappointment. I count myself among those that have survived financial setbacks. Although I may reference some of those examples I would rather help people focus on their own place in space and make that a better place to be on a daily basis.

How do we define our perception of how things work when we deny consideration of such ideas? We define our perception of

What is The Big Picture?

the world by what we do as we make an effort to succeed at just about anything we do. It could be something as simple as communicating with a friend. Do we send them a traditional letter through the U.S. Post Office or do we call them on a cellular phone? We may send an instant message or a "text" to communicate. Our action defines how things work in our world.

The same is true of our work and the jobs we hold over a lifetime of work. Do we show up on the door step of an established business and try to persuade the proprietor of our ability to do some particular job that has either been advertised or mentioned by someone familiar with the business? Are we instead seeking work from customers directly and going the extra mile to establish our product or service in a marketplace? Most people restrict themselves to what they are familiar with in most instances. This self limiting action can be very detrimental in a shrinking marketplace. Today's marketplace for jobs is more varied than it has ever been in the past. Technology has allowed virtually anyone to enter the marketplace at a minimal cost. The exceptions to this of course are licensing and credentialed jobs. Some of this is for the protection of the customer from unscrupulous business practices, but other instances are more political in nature and just plain protect the current job holders from competition.

Who are you and how do you perceive the world around you? If you needed work or more specifically a job how would you begin? Start by defining what you can do in a general way. Next, what are the specific skills you possess, and equipment you can operate? Ask yourself, do my efforts contribute to either a service or a product that a customer can buy? Cultivating skills that can be offered on a contract basis for either producing a product or for delivering a service will be of greatest value. If you were an auto worker that attached components to a vehicle on an assembly line you still have great value even if that specific job is not available today. As an individual you were probably expected to work with a team, so give yourself credit for coordination with other team members. You also had to work with specific tools that required some level of stamina and focus. I mention these things because they are a part of many other jobs that are just waiting for someone like you. Think product, think service. Many people buy things that require assembly, but once they buy it who is available to assemble it? Maybe you could be that person. Assembling a product that someone else sold, purchased and finally used is what many auto workers did for a living.

Remember assembly work is not limited to automobiles, Christmas gifts or any items for any season or specific part of the country. That means you can go anywhere and find assembly work. The problem is no one ever advertises their ability to assemble things and attaches a price to that service. This is an opportunity for people that want work. Auto workers are also available on several "shifts", days, afternoons, evenings and even midnights. If a customer saw your advertisement and asked when you were available I hope the answer would be, immediately! Maybe someone somewhere needs a swing set assembled for a birthday present the next day. Could you deliver a satisfactory assembly service? Maybe someone needs a bicycle assembled for themselves but hasn't a tool in the house. Could you do the job? Just like the automobile someone else sold it someone else bought it, and someone else was needed to assemble it.

Regardless of the automation that became a part of the automobile industry the work skills of people in the workforce are transferable to other products. One of the most recent examples in Michigan is that of a machine shop that made auto parts and had to shift production to windmill parts. They found another product to produce and they still employ machinists. Not all manufacturing industry can be as nimble as this one machine shop, but individuals that have been unemployed by the industry can have more options and flexibility because they do not have the same capital investments to consider. You might say my home and my family live in a community with few jobs available. I say consider non-conventional jobs that use conventional and even traditional skills. Be creative in the way you offer products and services to the community around you.

It is that moment by moment action that establishes new habits and job opportunities that will take an average auto worker and transform them into a small business person with great

What is The Big Picture?

potential. No one can establish the habits you will need to create a future full of promise but you. We are all creatures of habit so be careful in what you choose to do over and over, because it becomes a habit good or bad.

I personally know of people that have followed many job opportunities outside of their everyday work at an auto company. They have used the outside activity as extra income, as a backup plan to stay employed or as a transition into retirement. The jobs have been as varied as the people and their passions. Joe a computer programmer and project engineer maintained a farm with 60 or more head of cattle. Bill a fellow designer worked on contract for outside job shops. Bunny managed rental properties. William had a blueberry farm in northern Michigan. These are decisions they made during good times that served them during slow periods at their primary job, but what about those that did not have an alternate plan in place?

Exploring alternative jobs and work arrangements may be more limited after losing greatly, but it makes it easier to sift through what is possible. A person that has limited funds is not likely to buy property and start a business. A better choice would be to buy a single and most popular product at an extremely good price and turn around and sell it for a slight profit to the first person that can afford to pay you for the convenience of not shopping. This kind of retailing has gone on for centuries, if the business model worked that long it will probably continue to work for you. Certainly you need to cover all of your cost regardless how incidental they may seem to be, but you need to stay within the limits customers are willing to pay.

Communities that have been impacted by losses in the automobile industry and suffer from continuing high unemployment rates such as Michigan or more specifically the metropolitan area of Detroit do not seem like a friendly environment for the small business person. Nothing could be further from the truth. Although traffic may have lessened, small business people will find many customers that still have the price of a good value when it exists. It is in these environments that customers will explore alternate marketplaces. Garage sales, large

What is The Big Picture?

open air markets and advertised special items that present good value.

There are still pockets of prosperity in communities that are difficult for retailers due to the job market. Even though Michigan may have documented over fifteen percent unemployment it still has over 80 percent of the workforce at work. Today I heard Detroit had 29 percent unemployment. The community may have restricted their spending because they lack confidence in the future and what may happen, but they will still continue to spend money in ways that preserve their prosperity going forward. That means they will continue to do required maintenance, spend during holidays, spend money for seasonal changes look for good value on things they want but do not need.

Individuals that are unemployed in these environments need to focus on opportunities that are presented during these times that will not be there during more prosperous times. Shoppers looking for better value are not as numerous during prosperous times. Although large companies such as Walmart and Costco have leverage in these very same markets, they do not cover all products or all services and certainly they do not offer all product lines. Likewise they tend to buy items that can only be mass produced in foreign markets where production costs are lower. The services they offer are generally contracted to outside small businesses. This can serve as further guidance for those unemployed people that want to become a small retailer or service provider. Do not start with products that can be easily purchased inexpensively at a large retailer and become aware of how you can be a preferred contract source for these large retailers.

A visit to an open air market will help the uninformed spot what sells and what can be sold for profit by small retailers. A visit to the large retailers can help the small retailer understand how products need to be presented for customers that have high expectations for relatively inexpensive products. Our large and diverse marketplace offers tremendous opportunity.

If you are not inclined to be a buyer and seller of products consider selling a service. A weak market has created new opportunity for enterprising service providers that otherwise would not exist. There are some services that can be postponed or even avoided all together, but others are in greater need than ever. One good example of this is caring for the elderly. The costs of purchasing these services that have been provided by large business organizations can be enormous. Here is where an enterprising caregiver can organize a limited homecare business around many customers that exist even in financially troubled communities.

The service an unskilled individual is able to provide is limited due to licensing and other regulation, but many unskilled day care and general care options are in great demand especially when that same care provided by a larger organization is priced at the high end of the unskilled wage scale due to administration and insurance costs. Caregiver work for the elderly or handicapped is ever increasing as the population continues to age. Michigan is going to compete with Florida for the largest population of seniors over the next ten years despite the high unemployment numbers. Private contracting caregivers for home care can be a lucrative option for the unemployed auto worker.

Other jobs in the service sector that support what customers are looking for may be more competitive. Customers are looking for help with maintenance of their homes and automobiles, but small businesses are already organized to meet many of these needs at reasonable prices. Maintenance work generally requires the capital investment of skill and tools. For the unemployed unskilled worker it would require additional time and support to transition to this type of work.

The perception people have of the world and how they fit is cultivated, but people that have learned to cope with change can fit in almost anywhere over time. The part of the transition that is difficult is the speed that change happens. For people that have adopted a life long learning approach to life when faced with new challenges of learning will not require the time that some may need to accept a new direction even late in a work life. In stressed environments like Michigan speed of acceptance can make a critical difference.

Home related work in Michigan has been stagnant for most of 2008 but in early 2009 the flood of foreclosures has brought

What is The Big Picture?

bargain hunters out. Foreclosure purchases and newly set prices for new homes stirred activity in the home related businesses in general. Everything from nursery sales of plants to finish homes to furniture to fill them has improved ever so slightly. Likewise opportunities for home repair and maintenance has increased. Alternatives for workers displaced by this slow period are somewhat different than the displaced auto worker. Jobs in and around home building and sales has always been more of a subcontracting adventure. Skilled and unskilled have pooled into networks that hire people on a job by job basis. Speculative building projects have become extremely limited.

People in the home industry have in many instances retreated to other ways of making a living that still are growing in the same communities that building projects have been closed down in. Health care for the populations that have aged and have not moved out of Michigan, Florida, California and Arizona still are a source of new work for people that have fallen out of the home industry. Recent politics surrounding health care may have long lasting and a cascading affect on the industry based on the political decisions that are made over the next few months and years. Meanwhile it is an industry that has picked up people displaced from more than one industry.

Banking although still vulnerable to failures going forward was propped up early by the federal government. People displaced from some of the mortgage company boiler rooms are finding new work generated by the recent foreclosure market and limited new home sales. New home sales in the month of July 2009 for Macomb county Michigan jump 29 percent, although the price of homes for this same area has dropped approximately 30 percent over the last two years. The new car sales being generated by government subsidy programs are likely pulling forward sales from future sales much like rebate programs offered by the auto companies did in the past. Banking dislocation is not behind us and will likely continue into the future as banks uncover the bad debt that has been hidden in financial instruments months and even years ago. Bank failures have increased dramatically over the last year or so leaving bad debts in place while bolstering the balance sheets with money from the federal government. In 2007 five banks failed, in 2008 25 banks failed now in 2009 as of July 29, 2009 64 banks have failed, http://www.fdic.gov/index.html

Although the health care field has absorbed some of those seeking work from the banking sector, just as it has with auto workers and home related jobs, a consolidation of banks and a recent spur in auto sales and home sales both new and used has helped retain those still employed. What is curious is the number of financial institutions that have become classified as banks in an effort to backstop their holdings with the federal guarantee provided to all those institutions classified as banks under the FDIC rules. The federal government did this early on when people began runs on failing banks in 2008. The jobs lost at banks have not gotten much media attention probably because people working for banks regardless of their position from teller to bank president are not sympathetic characters among the unemployed. They are not viewed as victims of the financial collapse as are auto workers and workers in the home industry. Those unemployed by bank failures are somewhat ignored, but like all others they will find work again as they adjust their perspective on the job market and get a clear perspective on just what kind of work is available to do in the future. Most of those unemployed in the banking sector have basic skills that can be transferred to other segments of the job market especially if they take advantage of limited training that will reorient them to new job opportunities.

The same could be said for those people in the investment business. The second quarter of 2009 has brought a sharp recovery in equity prices in the stock market, but that hasn't necessarily translated into more work for those displaced by the financial collapse six months earlier. Instead the early recovery of equity prices prop up hope for a continued recovery that may take many more years not just months. The perception by those hoping for recovery is that recent improvement in stock prices is the first step in a rather long period of recovery. People inside the investment community are arguing both positive and negative direction going forward each point to the same recent history of stock recovery to bolster their argument.

What is The Big Picture?

When it comes to replacement jobs for investment workers they vary greatly like any replacement job because they depend on the limits and willingness of the individual. The perception many people have of an investment worker is that they sit in an air conditioned office studying facts and figures charts and financial statements. Some of that may be true but people in the investment business may spend enormous time on the telephone with clients or potential clients. They may spend time visiting companies and seeking businesses with potential that need seed money from new investors. They will expect return on the initial money invested. If you look at the many tasks that investors do as part of a larger task it is not difficult to find other businesses that can use these same skills.

It could be said that no matter what job you hold, an autoworker, a home builder, a banker or an investment worker the skills that you assemble into a skill set for accomplishing specific tasks can be fundamentals for accomplishing a larger set of tasks that can be applied to many different businesses. Certainly it is more preferable to stay on a familiar path that you may have followed for years, but spending time investigating a new path while you wait for other answers or leads to materialize can be time well spent. This is the "Big Picture". A world that can use what you have to offer, but depends on you to investigate the possibilities.

Before you think of some reason to debunk the theory that anything is possible consider the stories of immigrants that have come to this country with nothing but the clothes on their backs and unable to speak the language of this country fluently. They haven't all made it to the boardroom of top corporations, but the fact that most have found a way to make a living and that some have rose to those boardroom positions supports the rationalization that basic skills are a foundation for success in business. Another key to success is to consider that you are competent to be in business for yourself. If the only consideration is obtaining and holding a job you have set a goal that once accomplished has too little to drive you to the next step of success. If on the other hand the first consideration is "What business would I like to run?" before you look for a job, the next step toward that goal will

What is The Big Picture?

be in place even if you have not formed a strategic and complete plan on how to move past obtaining a job. The focus will be on the next step every step of the way creating a momentum and energy that can sustain you through trials and testing periods. You will find job hunting a far less stressful experience if you are less concerned with getting a particular job and focused more on a job that moves you into a position that teaches you something more about the business that you ultimately would like to run as a proprietor or as a manager. Most business people will tell you that the greatest lessons they have learned were not while sitting in a classroom listening to a professor, but instead somewhere along the road to success as they learned from the early failures that made them more successful as they made repeated efforts to move on to the next step in what may have seemed like a never ending string of failures.

We do not need to have all the answers before we begin our journey toward success, because the most valuable lessons to be learned are on the road to success not sitting in a chair contemplating the journey. So when I say "Jobs Will Happen" I mean jobs are only an incidental benchmark on the way to a far greater success that needs to be the focus of any individual that wants something more than one dead end job after another. Do not let the job, or the trappings of the job, be the focus of any effort. Instead focus on a continuum of successful efforts that will eventually lead to a successful business venture. This prevents you from settling for a job that does not contribute to a greater success over time. It also informs you that any job you take is only a single step in a much longer journey that can last a lifetime.

What is the "Big Picture" that sustains you during less than successful moments? Is that image constant or ever changing? One way to determine if the "Big Picture" you have is one that can lead to success is to determine if it connects with you and specific values you have. As you imagine some time in the future when you are more successful consider if it includes those things that sustain your effort today here and now. The only way that contemplating a more prosperous future can provide you with energy not found elsewhere is if it recognizes the specific things you value today. If you have a vision of a life that is so removed from what you value it becomes

What is The Big Picture?

an image with little energy and is rather worthless as a tool for moving past where you are today in the job you do to make ends meet.

Do a simple test. Create two images of somewhere in the future, one image connects with five things you value today and the other has absolutely no connection to anything you value. Now take some rather mundane task like washing clothes or dishes or grocery shopping and try to use the image to sustain a positive attitude as you work through any task of your choosing. The images that do not connect with you in a real way today will not sustain you. You will find your mind wandering and getting through the task difficult at best. Now take that image of the future that has a real connection with you and what you value and use it to sustain you through a difficult and rather routine task. Notice that your attention only shifts back and forth between the task and your image. The distractions that tend to sap your energy to get things done seem to fade in the background. Using simple images to maintain focus is used by young and old rich and poor to achieve success moment to moment, hour by hour and day to day.

This is how a "Big Picture" can help develop good habits that sustain long efforts to reach intermediate success and long term success. It is patience and persistence over time that will build a history that you can look back on for strength when things just don't work out. Remember, successful people usually have overcome many failures. Look at occasional failure as an opportunity to learn and adjust what you do to move in closer to that image of where you want to be. The details of where you want to be will be revealed over time so don't fail to act just because your image lacks detail. Some people will obsess over the detail just because they are a little bit more obsessive than average. Those that obsess should try to use it to strengthen their focus on the here and now and what detail needs to exist to be successful short term instead of trying to find the detail of a rather unsure future. I was reminded of this by a lady I had the pleasure to meet only over the telephone, her name is Temple Grandin. She has achieved rather great success as an architect of cattle handling equipment, but her success and ability to visualize the detail was limited to the detail of

What is The Big Picture?

the task in front of her. For her, words communicated large amounts of detail. If she used the words "Church Steeple" she did not have a fuzzy idea of what it looked like instead she could describe the detail and even the dimensions. This could have been a disadvantage. Instead, she applied this ability to visualize detail of what she knew to her cattle handling projects. She could do a virtual tour of facilities she had designed in her mind before she put the details on paper to describe them to someone else. Temple Grandin has been involved in the design of cattle handling in the United States, Canada, Europe, Mexico, Australia, New Zealand and other countries (http://www.grandin.com/temple.html). She is a professor at Colorado University and has written numerous books. Her accomplishments are significant, but when you consider she does all of this despite being autistic the accomplishments become even more significant.

Ordinary people, myself included, marvel at the accomplishments of exceptionally accomplished people, but more than that we gain a bit more resolve to carry on in a difficult environment. We may not have confidence in everything we do, but we are occasionally reinforced by success that is a result of many hours of effort. I have spent many hours in class rooms and on the job acquiring new skills and understanding that have helped me hold many jobs over a lifetime. I have found some of the best opportunities in times like we are experiencing today. The key to finding something positive to say about times when millions of jobs have been lost and trillions of dollars in investments have been lost is to understand that old practices of hiring people and of investing are being reconsidered in an attempt to squeeze profit and growth out of a stressed marketplace.

One such experience I had was as I approached my last thousand dollars of saving after being unemployed for nearly a year. I made the decision to try to sell my skills as a self employed designer on a contract basis. Ordinarily I was employed as an hourly employee of a larger company. Surprisingly to me my first contract paid for the initial outlay of $500 I had to make for equipment and space and lead to several years of employment that was not available to me before that commitment. While working as a

What is The Big Picture?

contractor many of the things learned during that period have served me well even today. When you work as an independent contractor the customer becomes your most valuable source of information.

The customers' "Big Picture" should influence our perception if we expect to be part of any marketplace. As a matter of fact we cannot escape the customers' view of things, because we are customers in many instances. As producers we tend to be more concerned with our burdens and not how our actions will impact the customers' opinion of the products and services we are engaged in producing.

During a down economy customers are highly sensitized to many aspects of a product that they do not consider during more prosperous times. Consideration of the product maintenance requirements, product warranty, retail return policy, rebates available and product place of origin are only a few of many. As you consider how things work in the world familiar to you, try to put some of the things you value as a customer in front of what you want as an employee. Here is an example, as a customer standing in a long line waiting to get waited on you as the employee may want to say this is my break time I am gone, but understanding the customer needs attention you call for additional assistance and stay until the customer lines shorten before you take a break. Customers notice small sacrifices and tolerate lines and waiting if it looks like the employees are working together to serve the customer.

A person without a job has a much better chance of securing their next job if they are customer focused and share that with any potential employer in interviews or casual conversation. Regardless of the business, employees and employers all serve the customer, and they all depend on returning customers to sustain and grow profits. The best employee is an employee that will build good customer relations in every action that they take. Ask yourself if a typical day for you includes consideration of the customer? If you are unemployed make daily customer consideration what prepares you for that first contact with the next employer. If you are employed daily customer consideration makes you a better and

What is The Big Picture?

more valuable employee every day you increase awareness of what customers expect.

It only takes the word of mouth of a few really satisfied customers to grow a business from a trickle of traffic to an overflow crowd. It is a bit discouraging to see employees in a prosperous business behaving poorly with customers, because you know that it is only a matter of time before the thriving business becomes a struggling business without a clue how things went wrong. Employees either consciously choose to find new ways to satisfy customers or they are doomed to discourage them over time. It is not as difficult as you might think to keep your customer in mind if all you do is consider yourself the customer of everything you deliver.

Don't let the customer priorities get turned upside down. Certainly a more perfect product or service is what the customer wants, but if you can't deliver in a window of time that satisfies the customer all else might not get considered. Think about those times you went to a restaurant and consistently were served good food, but constantly had to look for the wait staff to get refills or something as simple as another piece of silverware or a napkin. At some point the focus shifts from the good food to the poor service. Good restaurants usually have a strategy that does not depend on one server to make or break the experience. For that matter, car manufacturers, home builders, bankers and investment companies have many points of contacts with customers providing as many opportunities to draw them in as well as drive them away. That is just the nature of business that the employee needs to help the business get right.

Since small business provides 60 to 80 percent of all new jobs (http://www.sba.gov/advo/stats/sbfaq.pdf) it makes sense that the smaller the business the more important it is to pick the right employees. When people go job hunting they seem to dismiss smaller businesses thinking a large company is the place to get larger rewards, when large companies may regard any individual employee as less important than do small business that need people that can do a multiple of things to contribute in a meaningful way.

What is The Big Picture?

Job seekers should consider that a company can be as small as one person; this means if someone hires you on a contract basis you could be considered a one person company. Many benefits are available to small companies that are not available to employees receiving a wage. For people struggling to make ends meet the most important considerations when it comes to benefits of small business could be the cost of transportation related to the job or perhaps deductions from what you collect for any cost that goes into delivering your product or service. Other benefits exist but leave them to people that are looking at small business as a long term proposition.

Even those of you who are uneasy about self employment should not rule it out, because the opportunity for full time employment may come from a single instance of contract work for a larger employer. Self employment is an easy way to develop a "Big Picture" of how the world works between producers and consumers. You gain sensitivity to the customer while feeling the pressure to produce a product or a service that is aligned with a price set by the market on any given day. Even the smallest business becomes a customer at some point, and when it does you become aware of how the price of everything that is a part of production will impact the cost of your product or service and the profit you can expect to realize.

Even though a large percentage of small businesses fail they have much better odds than do lottery tickets and casino gambling. If you had a one in ten chance at walking into a job today how does that compare to the odds of finding a job that someone else has created and chooses you from thousands of other applicants? Your first job as a private business person does not need to be complicated. You only need to find something to do that anyone else is willing to pay you for doing. It can be a simple as collecting redeemable bottles and cans and walking them to an automated bottle return and collecting money at the cashier instead of paying the cashier. Maybe you only convince one person today to exchange the cans they have that may be worth ten dollars to exchange them for one dollar and the convenience of not making the trip to the store. Tomorrow you convince fifteen people of the same thing. By

What is The Big Picture?

the seventh day you have convinced some 50 or more people to do the same thing. That week you spent 18 hours talking to some 50 people over 6 days and paid each of them one dollar in exchange for 10 dollars worth of bottles and cans. You went to 25 stores one day later over seven hours returning a maximum of 20 dollars worth of bottle at each store. You collected 500 dollars for returning 5000 bottles and cans. If you subtract the 50 dollars you paid for the bottles you made 450 dollars over one week for 25 hours of activity. You made 18 dollars an hour for your effort. By the way do not forget to pay all the local, state and federal taxes on your income, because you are now a small business person. Remember you are allowed to deduct the cost of earning that profit from your activity which may only be the transportation and bag you carried the bottles in but it is more than if you only returned your own bottles and redeemed money you had originally spent when you bought the bottles and cans.

Business people are not necessarily brilliant people that come along once in a lifetime. They are instead people that see something that needs doing for a price and get about doing it without a lot of hesitation. Most business people work long and hard to achieve success, but they do not always feel that the work they do is objectionable or difficult, instead they enjoy what they do and often change what they do over time to meet the needs of the customer.

Stop and think about your world and how things work. Given the example of collecting bottles, could you come up with a similarly simple task that could net you some earnings that is likewise easy to calculate for one week worth of activity? Think about products and services that you have paid for on a regular basis. The more familiar you are with the item you select the easier it will be to calculate the weekly profit you can expect.

The "Big Picture" should not limit your possibilities' instead it should expand the limits of what is possible and what opportunity exists regardless of the state of the economy. The rules that govern the marketplace are not all made by government officials. All of those complicated rules and tax assessments are imposed on a marketplace that has unwritten rules that determine who prospers in business and who goes out of business.

Although many people make a living explaining the rules of the marketplace, you need only listen to successful business people that share what they know for free. Everyday in the media there are interviews with business leaders explaining their approach. Listen carefully to their success stories. Listen to how they continue to do business in a difficult business environment.

All businesses have fundamentals that make their model for profit making common to other businesses. Basic fundamentals like supply and demand, quality and pricing. These fundamentals can be interfered with by government regulations, but it only means the equation changes accounting for another variable. If regulations impose greater costs on business then business will adjust their price and pass the cost on to the customer. If price controls are put in place to prevent increases, then supply will dwindle and markets outside the reach of regulation spring up. Regulatory interference should be a way to protect consumers from bad business practices, but the good intentions of politicians usually have many unintended consequences.

How does all of that bureaucratic noise impact you and the job you want? Overall it may make it more difficult because of licensing and certifications that are required to even hold some jobs. It may even prevent you from working if the law does not recognize your right to work. You may live in an area that prevents employers such as large retailers from locating near where you live. Regulations vary from community to community and what is not allowed in one community may be allowed in another just a block away. Other factors that separate people that want jobs from jobs available may stem from poor planning and management of the politicians that had resources, but squandered them when times were good and have little or no resources to attract business when times are bad. If crime drives business away from where you live it may likewise drive you away for the same reason.

Despite all the difficulty business has in establishing and maintaining a thriving marketplace in any given community as a person looking for a job or for a marketplace to be a part of as another business you need only use a short checklist to identify the one place right for you. Is it a place that you can find transportation to and from every day? Is it a place where a variety of businesses thrive? Is there a mix of business, restaurants, retailers, small industrial firms? When the economy is good business can survive in very difficult environments, but when the economy is weak and business has small profit margins environment can be a critical difference between success and failure. People seem to have greater confidence in businesses in prosperous areas and tend to shop there even if the perception does not recognize failing businesses in the same community.

Much is written about cities and states that continue to do well in an economy that has destroyed other cities and brought states near default. If you choose to offer a product or service in a depressed area for any reason you should prepare to deal with problems not common to a more prosperous area. There are benefits that over time may out weigh the disadvantages. Without stating some of the more obvious disadvantages the advantages a depressed location offers are lack of competition, lower costs that allow for higher profit margins, but safety measures cannot be allowed to break the budget. Large depressed cities such as Detroit or Los Angeles have high crime figures that can take the profit out of a small business in one afternoon, but despite this some small businesses do find a way to prosper. Crime must be a consideration in any city an alternative to high crime areas might be neighboring communities that can provide a climate where business can thrive. This may only be a twenty minute drive from some of the worst crime areas of a large city.

For the person new to business many alternative and temporary sites can be had for a relatively inexpensive price. Around the country open markets are a place where people new to business can get started. The up front costs are low and you are officially a member of a legitimate market. Usually if they are in a high crime area they receive special attention by police and make it a better alternative than opening a lone storefront. If all you want is a job these same places may offer job opportunities short of setting up a space for yourself. It can be a way to get a better feel for the requirements of being successful as a business owner. You just might go shopping one day and be employed by the store where you shopped the next day.

Considering self employment needs to be a part of what anyone unemployed for extended periods of time considers. Some people that do not do well as employees thrive as small business people. A person that lacks the self discipline to maintain a job is not usually successful as a business owner, but sometimes being in business even a small business can give people motivation they never had before that time. Self employment for hard working and determined people regardless of their employment record in the past may be an experience that is life changing.

Self employment can be part of that larger vision that puts the individual in touch with a customer. Some people work at jobs all their lives without developing a feel for the ultimate customer of the product they have a hand in satisfying. As a job seeker how you view the customer can be the difference between short and long term employment. Having a larger perspective of how the customer supports employees such as you can be the difference between a successful business person and one that goes from one failed attempt to another. Even one person business establishments require a customer connection that satisfies many customers in a similar way over time. Learning how you can be a part of that customer satisfaction makes you both a better potential employee and a potential business person.

Why push self employment as a way to get a job? As a self employed person you will be less inclined to miss an opportunity to earn a living. Self employment may help avoid holding several part time jobs as an employee. As a small business person you may do a multiple of things to satisfy a customer and to earn payment by the customer, but you are always working at the same job, serving the customer.

Now that I have told you how great it could be to be a small business person let me share some of the realities of the day. Small businesses that did well when the economy was good are struggling to keep enough business to keep the doors open today. Why do they struggle? The customer is lacking confidence in the economy

What is The Big Picture?

and has pulled back on all types of spending. Small business has an advantage here over bigger business. Small business can quickly lower their spending and adjust to the marketplace. Unfortunately some markets have closed and the customers do not exist in certain geographical parts of the country. Small business in response has tried to reinvent itself. Some examples would be new car dealers that no longer can sell new cars are selling used cars only. Machine shops that made automotive parts now make parts for wind driven electrical generators. Retailers have had to expand the variety of offerings and be creative in their advertised sales in an attempt to satisfy more customers that are just spending less. Some small businesses have gone so far as to change their entire product line in search of a new customer base.

In the first half of 2009 business continues to adjust to all the new realities of 2008. Some small business is doing better than others, but it is reasonable to say that no small business is satisfied with the economy as it is today. As customers and businesses sort through a "house cleaning" of sorts that will eventually make customers and businesses more confident in their purchases the economy inches back from negative growth. When an economy as large as the United States is shrinking not growing creditors are more cautious limiting the purchasing power of both consumers and businesses alike. Often it is the business spending that helps jump start a stumbling economy this time around government has funded some spending to "prime the economy pump". Regardless of the large government plans they can never replace the spending that individuals and small businesses can contribute to any recovery. Some limited growth of business has returned in the early months of 2010.

Consider the opportunity to be a part of those that consider themselves small business people. If you are in small business and struggling to survive in the current economy try to recall the times when you had a passion to take on big challenges. Those challenges of the past were probably more about the just getting the job done not finding work to keep the doors open. Today a smaller marketplace for most commodities and services with few exceptions challenges us to consider how the skills we still possess apply to the few markets that have remained open and growing.

Wherever you are in the job market if a job is what you need take time to do the analysis that considers the many opportunities you have as compared to the loss of a single job. Even if you feel totally out of place as you seek work remember that staying focused on selling what you contribute to some product or service must be clear in your mind before you can explain it to a potential customer. Question your place in the supply chain of any product or service you want to be a part of so that when the customer raises the question you will have a logical answer. Ask yourself who am I to the customer. Think about your role as a person introducing yourself and the product or service you provide.

The personal touch that is not provided by any television commercial or advertisement needs to be present in the words you speak to the customer. Today unlike the past we have many more ways to reach the customer. A brick and mortar street address is only one place to establish a presence. If you do not have access to the internet you need to consider it as another place to locate a storefront or perhaps the first place to locate a storefront. It is usually inexpensive to setup a place where people can reach you and respond to any advertisement you provide. It makes you available to the world as compared to people that casually meet you in the physical marketplace. Some businesses are only present in this medium and do millions of dollars in business. For them a brick and mortar location is a waste of time and space. Internet marketplaces are flexible inexpensive and virtually available to anyone anywhere 24 hours a day.

So if you have introduced yourself to the world either in a small way at a local marketplace or over the internet think about the questions the customer may have when they consider services or products you offer. Compare your product or service to all others like it. Make your product or service as good as any other or better if you can. Give the customer as many ways to pay for your product as possible, cash, check, credit, or a third party service. Give your customer at least three ways to buy your product or service in person, over the telephone or over the internet. The "Big Picture" for you recognizes all other competition and welcomes them for comparison, because you know that any fair minded review of your product or service will rank yours' at the top end of any scale.

If people are unaware of your product or service take time to investigate inexpensive marketing before squandering all of whatever seed money you have on a marketing plan that may or may not work. If you start small and find a method of reaching customers that works for you do more of the same. Review the results of any marketing you do every day. Keep the approach fresh and do not be afraid to change what does not work in search of some one or two things that do work.

You are in charge of finding work for yourself, so do not be bashful when it comes to introducing yourself and what you provide for customers. You must sell your image to someone before you sell any other product or service. Remember there are 24 hours in every day and some efforts such as mailings to prospective employers or customers can be working for you while you spend time making contacts on the telephone. Although selling can be a job onto itself all work must be sold, so like it or not you must give some consideration to selling in your view of the world and how things work.

When you approach a customer you need to be able to describe what you have to offer in 30 seconds, because that may be the only time a potential customer is willing to give of their time. Practice what you need to say and say the most important things first. Consider before hand what questions they may have. You might have a friend pretend to be a new customer that has questions, just to test how you will respond.

All things are possible, but some things are more probable than others, so be a realist. Be positive, but expect to encounter setbacks on the way to success. Patience and persistence will serve you well on the way to the next job you will hold. Many temporary pieces of work put together are called long term employment. Do not minimize or think less of the smallest bit of work, because it could be the first of many opportunities at long term employment.

Chapter 2

Where Do I Begin?

S tart today, start here and now. Let me guess it is 8:00pm and you are tired after a long day of looking for work. If that is true just remember that the day is young. You need rest and sleep, but you need to prepare for tomorrow today no matter how late it is prepare for tomorrow. Consider where you will go, what you will do, and who you will see then ask yourself why? If you are unemployed 80 percent of the time you spend during working hours needs to be connected to finding the customer that is going to help you pay for all those things you want and need in life.

Make the remainder of this day, a day of action. Tomorrow will be a day of discovery. The analysis and plans you make today will be met by the reality of tomorrow and the combination will yield a new direction based on what you learn. Reconciling the plans you make with what actually happens should not be a disappointment, but instead instructive. You may not learn big lessons, but you must seek small lessons that can redirect you onto a path that leads you to that job you seek. Remember the job will happen if you focus on taking steps everyday that take you closer to people that provide work. Knowing the customer of any business is the first consideration, and knowing more about how businesses that interest you serve people is next.

Start with making a list of the customer preferences you have regarding any product or service you use on a daily basis. The daily encounters are usually foremost in our mind and easiest to recall. The preferences you have will match those of many other people. Ask friends or acquaintances to identify some of their preferences and see how many match yours. Keep track of the number of duplicates, because you will use them to identify the highest ranking preferences. Think of the top ten on the list as things to do when you serve someone in the least of ways.

A second list is that of top complaints, and these should serve as a list of actions to avoid. We all tend to separate our experience as a customer from our experience as a provider. Bringing the two together will tend to make you both a better customer and provider. Go back to that plan of things to do for the next day, can you see opportunities to improve yourself as a customer or as a provider of a service or product in any of those things you have planned to do tomorrow? Now that you have put together a plan for tomorrow you can think about getting some sleep, but not before you consider one more thing. What is the eating plan for tomorrow? Eating plan? Yes eating plan!

One of the most overlooked features of any plan for work is how we take care of the person expected to do the work. Now by this I mean a lack of planning usually leads us to poor nutrition and generally poor eating habits. Did you know that if you improve your plan for eating it will not only make you feel better about waking up in the morning and going to work, but also help you work longer and stronger? You will also look healthier to customers and prospective employers.

First appearances are important so start by considering what you typically have for breakfast lunch and dinner. Next consider that what you have in the first meal must give you energy to get you going. Here is a suggestion for the first meal, include some protein either liquid or solid, milk or eggs, minimize the fat, low fat milk or three egg whites for every whole egg. Include some high fiber low calorie bread and minimize the butter you use. You can substitute meat for your eggs, but try to keep it low in fat. Ham is better than bacon and a lean beef is better than both. Try to avoid including things like pancakes or waffles or generally any sweet foods. Include tea or coffee if you choose, but here again avoid adding sugar or cream in excess.

This is not a diet, but it is another key to securing that next job. If you consider the days that have lead up to today and some of the stress you have encountered along the way ask yourself if the food choices you have been making lately have been good ones? The answer is probably no. This needs to change on the first day you get serious about getting that next job, because you are going to need more energy and more stamina to get through each day going forward. If you look healthier to the employer and sound energetic and ready for any challenge you are a better choice for that reason alone. The employer needs someone they can depend on regardless of what role you will have in the business. Being alert and energetic is one of several things most employers look for in a new hire.

Employers even at some of the largest companies have made fitness for work part of what they consider. Small businesses that have a lot of people to choose from with only a few positions to fill can be picky. All employers consider the demands of the job against the person that sits before them looking for employment. Even if you have been unemployed for some length of time, if you look fit for work and sound energetic you could be the choice they make.

Likewise if you are considering self employment the customer will think very similar to the employer. They are just as quick to match your first appearance with what they expect. The expectations most people have of business people is driven by their best experience. In other words if they bought something from a business and enjoyed what they bought that image becomes a good experience they are looking to repeat. It is the reason successful businesses have many repeat customers. Customers want to repeat that good experience over and over. Make an effort to be the next good experience someone has tomorrow.

Do not let the opportunity of tomorrow be postponed by a lack of planning today. Begin each day with a plan different than the day before, because no two days are the same. Make consideration of today and how things went a part of why you plan what you plan for tomorrow. Let each success no matter how small be the spark that keeps you taking the next step on a never ending journey to achieve something more than just a job or a paycheck. Let your success enable you to think more about the future than the past. Be the first one to recognize the errors you make, so you can be quick to rectify them before they cost a customer the pleasure of working with you.

When you decide the day is over, avoid falling asleep in a chair if you can. Go to bed and make yourself comfortable for tomorrow comes all too soon and you will need a good nights sleep to meet the challenges of tomorrow. Adjusting your eating and sleeping schedule while looking for a job might seem a bit disconnected, but it is all about preparing you for a successful job opportunity. When I was younger like so many others I ignored the connection between preparing for a job interview and my expectations of success. Needless to say many opportunities were lost. On those occasions when I did get the job I was a little less than prepared for what it might take to keep the job. The first time the world of work tested my ability to make hard decisions, develop and execute a workable plan to save my job I was 19 years old. There were all kinds of excuses for why work and required schooling had conflicted, but the bottom line was that other employees were performing fine under the same conditions. I was told at a formal meeting of the same people that had hired me that I had one week to put together a plan to correct my poor performance and sell it to the plant manager or consider my job lost. This was a four year program that I was only one year into and I had let poor eating, sleeping and work habits threaten my ability to earn a good living for the foreseeable future. Fortunately the plan I came up with was accepted and I did execute it with more success than even I had anticipated. After two to three weeks of intense focus on what needed to be done and working one day at a time to accomplish limited goals I was back to a performance level that met or exceeded all requirements. Unfortunately several other students in my class that had not been as successful were asked to leave.

The odd thing about that experience was that it introduced me to a new element of the job that lead to a new four year program after completing the first program with even higher pay and greater satisfaction. The second program was not easy and was quite competitive, but yielded many job opportunities afterwards. It might seem strange that adversity provides some of the best chances to escape old ways and bad habits, but when you come to a crossroad that gives you a choice between continuing bad habits that are self destructive and forming new habits that lead to health and prosperity you need to decide. Today there is adversity all around us, the work environment is stressed as greater productivity is called for and the unemployed are being asked to learn new skills before they return to work. The marketplace for work has contracted and the way work is accomplished has changed significantly over only the past year. This is on top of significant changes in technology over the past ten years or more. How do we refocus on personal goals that support us in an environment of change and pressure to perform better?

Consider that all business large and small is made up of many people doing a job that contributes to a product or service a customer needs or wants. Secondly, that the same product or service will be compared to many like it over time in the same market and it may or may not be competitive. Ask yourself, are you focused and prepared to contribute to a competitive product or service? What do you do every day to communicate that readiness to the people you come in contact with either in a job search or in everyday routines? It is not always what you say that makes a lasting impression as it is what you do. Every time you set out to satisfy someone try to think of a way to top it off in a way that makes what you provide extra special. Many employees deliver the same basic product, or service; some employees just give that extra measure of consideration. Are you the kind of person that would give extra consideration?

The market for all products and services has fallen from all time highs to moderate and less than zero growth in some instances. If all business had an equal share of healthy and productive people then the chance of someone new getting a job would be low. Some businesses are hopelessly full of unproductive people. Businesses use the cover of a bad economy to eliminate the most unproductive portion of their workforce. This does create opportunity for more energetic and capable people to replace them. Some companies even during the best of times routinely replace ten percent of their workforce every year. If you are looking for steady work and a considerate manager give self employment another look. Self employment operates with less structure and generally demands more of you than would anyone that might hire you as an employee, but it can also be very satisfying to have larger base of support than a single company.

The rules to be self employed are easy to follow. If you consistently take in more money from sales than you spend providing that product or service you can succeed. Some businesses

Where Do I Begin?

have higher profit margins than others, so if you are interested in business think about the details of one that interests you. First and foremost the business should be something that you have some understanding of be it simple or complex. People that have been unemployed and are seeking jobs are not always in the best position to start a business, but there are many exceptions to that rule. First consideration for low budget business is to consider establishing a cash flow. You must generate sales before you spend anything more than the price of a three line advertisement in a local newspaper. Is the product or service something you can produce with the money you have on hand? If it requires capital that is beyond a personal loan from someone you know the planning and risk increase exponentially. Although some of the most successful business models are those of franchised businesses they are likewise usually well beyond the means of an unemployed person with few resources.

Self employment can be limited, supplemental or the only thing you do for a living, but you decide what level of self direction is right for you. Some people feel uncomfortable with the lack of structure and the level of discipline that is needed from time to time. Other people feel totally liberated and after experiencing the freedom that self employment offers they strive to make it a full time pursuit.

Most successful people will tell you of the many less than satisfying jobs they worked at only because it was a means of sustaining them when the next step was not clear. Despite any plan to succeed everyday life has a way of detouring us along the way. The most successful people understand that this is only a detour and persist in an effort to find their way back on to the road to success. Less successful people become all caught up in the detour and emotionally stuck in place longer than necessary; when what they needed to do was accept the detour for what it was and keep taking positive steps that are likely to lead to a greater success.

Selling has many detours and many setbacks; probably this is the reason few people choose to take a job as salesperson. The people that are better acquainted with the sales environment understand that buyers are only a small percentage of any market.

Where Do I Begin?

For a person accustom to having the largest percentage of their work accepted by an employer this can be a bit depressing. An employee that learns to build quality into their work everyday usually is praised on a regular basis. As a salesperson the praise of an employer or customer may take time to develop. People uncomfortable with selling need to understand that like it or not they sell to someone everyday. Even if you are not presenting a product or service you are presenting how you engage the work of getting through the day.

Do you approach the routine tasks you need to complete with energy, purpose and determination to get it done? Any casual observer will use this as your presentation for how you may approach a job for them. Present yourself in everything you do as a person that can be counted on to work through the difficulty of a task to completion. One rather famous Chief Executive Officer at General Electric, Jack Welsch in his book Winning 2005, narrowed it down to what he called "the four E's plus passion". For him if you had "Energy, could Energize others, an Edge or the ability to decide and the ability to Execute a plan" you were among those candidates worth consideration. Now how could anyone tell that much about a person from a resume or a job interview? Well resumes and job interviews are not what they were years ago. Today asymmetric interviews that ask more about a persons approach to situations rather than about their past experience tend to provide prospective employers with some idea of how you would perform in their work environment.

For a person not interested in a sales job consider the interview a test of your ability to sell yourself. Presenting a product or service may take some skill beyond that, but all sales people must sell themselves first and foremost. Like the prospective employee a sales person does best when they establish a personal connection with prospective employer. That does not mean being casual in the approach you take to the interview, but instead picking up on how the interviewer presents themselves and respecting and reflecting that approach to the interview. For example if the interviewer asks how you got to the interview they may be interested in the means of transportation you have available. If a friend gave you a ride to the interview say so, but include how you plan to get to work on a daily basis. If the interviewer seems interested in how you are doing in your job search, be positive and include the reason you selected this request for an interview.

Selling can be an exciting experience that may provide new opportunities for you not available as an employee. Some sales people have developed a network of contacts that makes them especially good at finding just the right product for the customer. Even when many products could satisfy the customer the sales person presents a range of products that allows the customer a choice that fits their personal needs. Keep the customer in charge of the decision of what to buy while coaching them on what the market has to offer other customers with similar needs. We all have stories of sales people that turn us off as customers. There are sales methods that can be effective short term, but they are not what we should use to sell ourselves if we are looking to develop a lasting connection with either a customer or employer. Some sales techniques that apply to closing sales are fair, because they help the sales person sort between customers ready to buy and some that would shop endlessly. Customers in search of the best bargain or with no real intention to buy may not want to reveal what will close the sale. Smart salespeople recognize this and generally drop the customer from consideration when the customer communicates they are not ready to buy. Smarter salespeople will at the same point lay out a best deal for the customer and let the customer think about it and move on to the next customer.

Countless books have been written about successful sales techniques by successful sales people. This is not one of those books. Instead I mention sales, because as a job seeker you cannot avoid having to sell yourself to someone. As a small business person likewise nothing happens until you sell a customer a product or service. Being aware of the selling component in any market is a fundamental part of achieving even the most limited of goals. During economic times such as these the selling part of getting a job or a customer is more difficult than ever so just understand that you need to spend more time sharpening sales skills in a poor economy with a marketplace that is tougher than it was only a year ago. For employers that need help they can be more cautious in picking their next employee. Remember that small business depends on only a few employees to do many things right. Likewise customers are hoping to get the quality they could not afford in a booming economy. Customers will spend money if they think there are exceptional buys to be made even during a poor market.

When you wake up do you start the day with a purpose in mind? Does that plan you worked on last night seem reasonable and realistic or do you say to yourself, "What was I thinking." No matter how it strikes you when you take a second look, be determined to get some part of it done today. Why not all of it? Well if you are not accustomed to making a daily plan and working it consistently start by accomplishing some part of the plan. You are not a fortune teller so don't be surprised if any day works out slightly different than you plan everyday. Work to accomplish small objectives that will lead you to a goal over time.

As a scheduler I made and saw many a plan. Success usually came from the simplest of plans that depended on new approaches to getting the job done and realistic benchmarks to improve performance. Keeping your daily plans simple to accomplish means they have clear and measurable objectives that move you in the direction of your goal. When do you need new ideas? The answer is when the ideas you are using do not give you the results you want or expect. There is never only one way to get something done. Trying new ways may not only get something done that did not get done, but may do it in far less time than you had expected. Once we start to accomplish objectives that lead to our goals we need to establish benchmarks that give us confidence. A benchmark is nothing more than a measure of what it took to get something done. Measure the time, measure the resources, and document the method so the next time you want to get something done you can predict with some accuracy what it takes to get it done. Although all plans need adjustment they help avoid making to many decisions as you do the work. If you approached all work without a plan your progress would be slow and your learning curve would be slow. We improve our performance by planning and adjusting those plans as things change. If there is a down side to planning it could be that you get so consumed with the plan and unrealistic expectations that the plan consumes too much time and not much gets done. The only successful plan is a plan that leads to accomplishing objectives and goals.

If you are looking to get a job or looking to be in business, providing a job for yourself and maybe a few other people, the work that lies ahead is not as difficult as you may think. The thing that will get you through most of what needs to be done is patience and persistence. If you are not a patient person just be willing to work harder and longer everyday to accomplish each step toward your goal. If you are not a persistent person use your plan to keep you engaged and working on each step that needs to be complete before moving ahead toward your goal. Many people with good jobs or with successful businesses are short on patience and may be just lucky not persistent. However if you cultivate both patience and persistence or some way to compensate for your lack of either, you are destined for success. How can I say that; am I a fortune teller? No, but any review of the most successful people in our society will reveal patient, persistent people that work toward a goal with a purpose. Your plan should identify your goal and a purpose for doing what you do in clear terms.

The source of your motivation may very over a wide spectrum. You may not be driven by some single burning desire that some people refer to when asked how they accomplished the goals they have had in life. Certainly having some larger purpose for doing what you do is preferable, because it helps stand in for other reasons that may seem less important as you experience life. If you have not discovered a purpose let your daily needs and wants drive your effort. Use real needs like housing, food, clothing that do not go away as are ability to earn improves. Transportation could also be included in that group of needs, because you need it to get to and from a job or a business. You may want a better grade of housing, food, clothing, or transportation and that may get you to work the overtime that pays for the upgrade.

Where to begin is different for everyone, because we each come to the job hunt with a unique history. Where you start should not discourage you. People achieve at different rates of speed. If you notice someone from similar circumstances making better progress than you seem to be making ask them how they accomplished their goal in such short time. Most people are flattered that you would ask and are more than happy to share their experience with you. Perhaps your plan is different for good reason, but you may be able to modify your plan to improve your success similar to more successful people. Never be afraid to ask questions that may educate you to a new approach that gets results.

Without anyone to compare yourself to the competition doesn't get easier instead it becomes you against the rest of the world. Be quick to identify some of the advantages you have over many other people in the world. Make the disadvantage an advantage. If you live in a disadvantaged area chances are that most people with any money to spend will spend it elsewhere, because products and services are not available in their neighborhood. If you can offer a product or service to those same people they may see an advantage to avoiding travel cost and time. If you live in an area where no one would think of using a shopping service, because retailers are in the neighborhood, visit the retailers and offer to be an on-call employee. It will minimize the employers' commitment and increase the chances of your employment. Considering new ways to do the same old thing can be the difference between early success and a late start.

If you are poorly educated and have only held manual labor types of work consider learning what is most obvious to the employer or customer you approach. Do they see a poorly dressed person? Do they hear someone that uses slang? Do they hear someone that lacks energy? These are all places to start. Use a person you admire to help you change your appearance. First impressions are important and may not be difficult to change with the right coaching. As you change your appearance employers will quickly assign new value to you as an employee. After being unemployed for several months while I was young I decided I would apply for a job as a dishwasher. Although all my previous work was semiskilled or skilled factory work the only jobs available were in restaurants at the time. When I applied for the job the

Where Do I Begin?

manager said something I will never forget, "You don't look like a dishwasher, maybe you could work as a cook?" Unfortunately I did not ask if he was willing to train me instead I insisted on the dishwasher job which I promptly quit at the first opportunity just as the manager had predicted. The job as cook paid about twice what I got as a dishwasher, but at that time I wasn't open to anything else. The manager saw something in me that I did not see in myself. Confidence in your ability to learn new things can be a valuable thing, because without it the path to success can be long and slow.

Some years later after much training and having far greater confidence I applied for a job as a designer. The manager was going to hire me, but had a question? Did I have any experience with transmission design for special machines? Well my experience was limited when it came to gear ratios and all the calculations necessary to develop a transmission, but I really wanted the job. I decided to tell the manager the truth about my experience, but insisted with some assistance I was sure I could learn what I needed to know. He thanked me for being honest about my background, because many applicants before me were not so forthcoming. Unfortunately he would not be able to hire me because he needed someone to lead the effort.

There is a place and time when things do come together and lead to a better day. Don't spend a lot of time beating on yourself for what happened in the past. Get busy today building what will be a successful effort to either get a job or get a business. You have the luxury of chasing either option or both options simultaneously. Spend the energy you have today on getting done the things that will make a difference tomorrow. Some of the things that will help you going forward include education, training, certification and general knowledge about the business activity that is prosperous in your local area. Give yourself an energy boost by improving how you take care of your health. Good eating habits, good activity schedule will move you in that direction.

What decisions have you made that will improve how you feel and appear to the people you will be approaching for a job or their business? Are the decisions you have made recently likely to add energy to your pitch to an employer or customer? Making good

Where Do I Begin?

decisions before you start looking for a job will help you make better decisions when you get a job or first customer of your new business. When you go out to look for a job or customer remember that people you meet have a family and friends. Even if they are not interested in your offer today perhaps they will share their good experience with family or friends that will contact you. If you can energize others by leaving a good first impression you may benefit from their network of family and friends. When you get a job or a customer be sure to satisfy that person by executing your job duties or delivering the product or service.

The difference between being the first choice and the runner up can be very small. If you are to be chosen for a job or selected by a customer you will be number one. Coming in third fourth or twenty-forth will not get you the job. After consideration of product, price, placement and promotion it is not enough to be in the running. Understanding this should help you focus energy on the first impression you make on people you meet. Many jobs today will take more than one interview, but that first impression goes a long way in establishing your value to the company or customer.

One way to understand the employee employer relationship is to consider that first and foremost the business is expecting to get more value from you than they are willing to pay you. The difference between what you are worth and what you are paid is what the company calls gross profit. If they contribute to you for sick days, vacation, health care, education and other costs they must subtract those from that gross profit. Initially most businesses would like to charge the customer twice what it cost them to pay for all your costs. With that in mind it is easy to see why self employment can be a profitable arrangement. The problem many self employed people have is rigorous accounting of time and expenses. The result of poor accounting is working for about half of what you could make at a job working for someone else.

When I say accounting I am not talking about fancy computer systems or high priced services. I am talking about keeping track of simple expenditures that become a part of any product or service you may provide. It is a little like keeping track of what you eat by writing it down throughout the day to avoid overeating. Likewise recording the money you spend throughout the day when expenses occur helps get control of spending when you are trying to make a profit. At the end of any day when you are making plans for tomorrow considering what food you ate or what money you spent can provide valuable insight for tomorrows plan. Forgetting the past extravagant spending and eating habits is easier said than done. Using a simple behavior modification technique of rewarding your good behavior and noting but avoiding rewards for bad behavior can help you change behavior day by day.

Regardless of where you start on your quest for a job having a positive attitude toward making change that will translate into a job is necessary. Start each day with some activity as well as a meal. Every day is a new effort to overcome the easy option to sit and wait for someone to come to you. The odds of someone seeking you out, without you publicizing what you can do for them, is probably worse than buying a lottery ticket. Even if you make a less than robust effort make some effort that keeps you under consideration by someone each day. Do not overlook your potential to establish a business that offers a simple product or service at a reasonable rate. If you land a part time job use the remainder of the time looking for something to fill the remaining hours.

Build rewards into your daily plan. If you have identified six things to do that day stop when you are half way through and sit down if only to enjoy the weather. Giving yourself simple rewards that are inexpensive on a regular basis for routine accomplishments will keep you moving in a positive direction. If something goes wrong and the day ends long before you have been able to accomplish much of anything, spend a little extra time reviewing what went wrong and how it might have been avoided before planning what you need to do tomorrow. Remember that the current economic environment may decline further before a market for you and what you have to offer is robust. Developing foraging habits that yield small rewards on an intermittent basis may be the best that can be accomplished for some time to come.

Good habits that get you through the day will preserve the potential you have by exercising your mind and your body for the foreseeable future. Falling pray to bad habits that either, squander the few resources you have or jeopardize your health will make you less competitive against an ever increasing number of unemployed people. Spending time during the day doing something that you enjoy and that hones the skills you have will be time well spent. If you have few resources seek public places like libraries and parks to spend free time instead of shopping malls and eateries. Even when you return to full employment you will find that the time you spent in public places will serve you well as a place you can return to relieve the stress of a busier life.

Instead of considering the totality of what you may have lost in a rather short span of time try to celebrate the limited gains you make on a daily basis. Comparing your situation to someone that is prosperous is not very comforting, but today it is easy to look around and find people that have suffered great loss of either fortune or health far beyond our own. Be comforted that the situation of some of the far less fortunate are not your plight. Go one step further and contribute in a small way to some of the organizations that help them. If you cannot contribute money contribute time or effort. You might wonder, what does this have to do with finding a job? Helping those less fortunate than you usually helps give you a better perspective on the work you face as you look for a job. It helps sustain the routine daily grind of seeking out work. It is another place to begin when what you need is work.

Consider some of the least likely places to begin as well. Starting out at the top of an organization seems unlikely, but if you are self employed you are the person in charge. When the market for all goods and services is deteriorating, how does a new business find customers? As a new business you have an opportunity to offer the same old customers better goods and services at a better price. Part of the reason many businesses suffered great losses was the inflated price they put on the goods or services they offered and if they are quick to adjust the price they have a better chance of staying in the market. If you recognize a large difference between the price of a product or service and its' value, would you wait for a better price? Likewise, customers that have sustained large losses in their assets are not likely to wait for an old business to change their unreasonable prices. Be the business to offer the customer savings

Where Do I Begin?

and value before others and you may have customers you did not expect.

Even if job loss totals are in the millions, the economy produced about 14 trillion dollars of goods and services in 2009. You need to increase what you produce to secure your future. Decide what part of that gross domestic product you will produce for a customer. Some improvement in the economy will make room for you if you have a plan. Considering what may be possible is a much more positive approach than simply letting the fact that millions of people are unemployed and will continue to be unemployed for some time to come be your only focus. When 10 percent of the population is unemployed 90 percent is still working and you are more likely to be among the 90 percent if you are truly interested in learning what makes you employable. Some particular demographic populations may even have 30 percent unemployed, but here again there is still greater odds of being employed than unemployed if the goal of the individual is to get employed.

So many times people that are unemployed accept the position too willingly. These are people that you will not have to worry about standing ahead of you applying for the next job. Like the unemployment numbers the number of people content with unemployment is a small percentage. This means that well paying jobs advertized with few requirements will probably have long lines of people anxious to apply. For the jobs that do not pay quite as well and require more initiative than they do experience will probably have shorter lines. For jobs that do not pay as well and require initiative and inventiveness and a willingness to work long and hard for improved benefits may not have anyone standing in line. As important as it might be to get back to enjoying life, give consideration to enjoying some part of the work.

When you have had a serious setback in the way you make your way through life it is probably a good time to rethink what you do to make things happen for you and others that depend on you. If you enjoy some part of what you do it usually makes working longer and harder a bit easier. The enjoyment you get from the work you do also has a way of finding its' way to the customer that appreciates the effort you put into your work. Do not refuse all

Where Do I Begin?

other work holding out for that one fairy tale job that you have always dreamed of, instead work at what is available always making time to consider other options as they present themselves. Some people think that working a job that does not satisfy you keeps you in a rut of work with little satisfaction. Actually the opposite is probably true, that is to say if you stay engaged in meaningful work at some level opportunities are more frequently available. It is not easy to pursue your dream job while working without much satisfaction. Only initiative, inventiveness and willingness to work long and hard will satisfy immediate and long term goals. Patience and persistence of the individual that has taken the time to identify what they want will make it happen.

At the beginning of any adventure there exists perhaps a plan with some short term objectives that will be tested and adjusted over time. Why not make the adventure worth looking forward to by establishing some objectives and goals that will improve your life upon completion? The entire journey may have started out as an unintended consequence of unpredictable circumstances, but when you start to take control results change. Opting to stay adrift with no plan will put you at greater risk of more of the same results. Your effort must begin to set multiple objectives that can all be worked together while striving for that ultimate goal of a job or business that sustains you. By improving several areas of your life simultaneously small gains in any one area will seem greater as they are achieved in harmony with one another. When we improve our health while working to improve our education that then helps us get the next job it all seems so much more satisfying than considering any one of those things on its' own.

We need to celebrate the small achievements as they occur to reinforce the good habits we build one day at a time. Rewarding good behavior while picking your self up off the floor when you stumble into bad behavior that brings you down is a simple strategy that may be difficult to establish. We all ignore or deny our own faults to some extent. It is not helpful to be down on yourself, but if you are failing to achieve objectives because you ignored to many bad habits it is not helpful to make endless excuses for your

Where Do I Begin?

behavior in an attempt to feel better about yourself. Let us not go back in history further than what happened yesterday. If we expect to make progress toward any goal we need to keep our focus on the present or the future for the sake of correcting errors, and use past successes to help sustain our effort. If you make an error today it becomes a learning experience and an adjustment in your plan for tomorrow. If you have succeeded in the past, but are off balance and without accomplishment today, look back on the success you have had big or small and use it to encourage a new effort today. Celebrating success sometimes needs to happen while you are experiencing a streak of failure to remind you that success is still a real possibility.

Indulge yourself in a vision of how your effort today will lead to a better life in the future. Having a better picture of where you want to be as compared to where you find yourself today can be a way of motivating consistently better habits that get you to your goals. Review your vision of where you want to be daily, because it like so many other things may change as a result to what you experience. Instead of trying to define the detail of your vision consider how realizing it will make you feel. Try to take time to imagine achieving your dream and the sense of accomplishment you would have at that time. Use those good feelings to energize what you need to do today to make your dream a reality.

The difference between achieving a vision of where you want to be and being stuck and hopeless in part depends on your ability to make decisions. Secondly you must make good choices when you do decide. It is understood that all decisions may not be good, but being able to decide quickly, and then working in that direction until the next decision is called for is very important. Some people spend too much time analyzing endless information in an attempt to make the very best decision and in effect decide through their inaction to deal with what other people decide. Gain control of where you are going and the results you expect by making timely good choices that reflect your thinking.

It is important that you quickly identify how much time you have to decide and make the best choice you can within the time allowed. It may be a prospective employer that needs to know how soon you can start working, or it may be a customer wondering how long they will need to wait for service. Even if the decision and the answer you give requires more from you to make it happen you must decide in a timely way with an answer that addresses the question and does not leave the employer or customer wondering. Successful decision making usually leads to that next step of making good on expectations of the employer or customer. It is always better to be able to deliver a quality product or service before it is expected. Avoid letting time run out on the estimate of time you give a customer, because all else about the product and service gets greater scrutiny.

Customers I had as a contract designer were usually impressed with my ability to deliver what they needed quickly. What customers did not see were the hours spent through the day or evening working to satisfy their request for a quick delivery. After picking up an order that was needed on an urgent basis I customarily would work 12 to 16 hours a day to complete the work. This came from years of working long hours in a job shop environment that was geared to complete contracts on a competitive basis. Some of the best people in the system competed among themselves to improve efficiencies. If someone said they had completed the job in 75 percent of the time allotted the next job was sure to be done in less time. The competition was usually friendly and made the work more interesting, because you were always striving for best practices that would yield equal or improved results in less time.

Customers of all products and services generally appreciate innovation that improves the delivery of products and services. Home delivery of everything from pizza to clothing has been born out of a customer request. Businesses looking for some way to improve their revenue in bad times have many times looked to satisfying a customer desire for convenience. Most recently I was both surprised and pleased to know that a local lawn equipment store would come to my home and do the annual maintenance on my lawn mower in their truck out in front of my home. There is some premium to the cost of the service, but it is a service I as a customer appreciate.

Where Do I Begin?

Think about the time when photographs needed to be developed in a laboratory with chemicals. Today you can take the photograph and print it out on a desktop printer. Certainly there are degrees of quality with the change in delivery, but matching the quality with the price puts the customer in charge of the decision. Unknown to the customer some photographic studios use the same retail stores for printing finished pictures as the customer could use themselves. Similarly construction contractors will rent tools and equipment from retail outlets to avoid the capital investment in expensive infrequently used items. The thing that cannot be found at the retail store is the expertise to know when such a match is appropriate. That is the difference between the do it yourselfer and the professional that matches the service to the job without degrading the product presented to the customer.

As you consider where to begin either looking for a job or looking for a customer consider that you need to start with the things you are most familiar with to ensure you have some confidence in a stressful situation. What has your life experience been? Have you had to care for people? Have you been asked to house sit property? Have you cared for someone's animal while they were gone on vacation? These are things you may have done as a favor for someone that could be turned into full time work. If you have some specific skill like repairing automobiles or bicycles or mending shirts it all can be translated into a higher wage. If the only thing you have ever done is clean your own living space, consider doing the same thing for someone other than yourself. Another consideration is laundry work coupled with a pickup and delivery service. Even during a recession there are people still willing to pay for certain conveniences.

Your long term goal can be as extravagant as you want to make it, but you need to quickly identify some practical places to begin. I won't guess at what long range goals you may have but only suggest that starting at the lowest step on a staircase that leads to that goal is no disgrace. Having a depth of experience usually works to your advantage not disadvantage. Even if you accept work that is unrelated to the long term goal you have do not let it keep from looking for other opportunities that might give you more satisfaction. It is the person that is less persistent and less patient that becomes frustrated with small but positive steps. If you stay positive and learn to motivate people around you with your optimism you will find that they will usually return the favor helping to bolster your persistence and patience. Just as I have discovered new directions to take I have shared them with others that have followed on behind having been encouraged by my success. Sometimes sharing the frustration you have overcome with someone else that seems to be having that same experience will be just what they need to move forward. Learn to share your success by training others to use what you have learned or how they might approach their challenge. Training others tends to test how thorough your understanding of the subject is while giving you insight into other practical alternatives. So start small and check your progress by discussing your progress with others interested in a similar path. Find practical ways to accomplish small objectives on your way to accomplishing larger goals.

Some of my fondest memories are of the people I met along the path my work life took me. I met some very talented people and noticed that their talent only grew stronger as their capacity for working harder and smarter than the next person increased. Some people that lacked the talent had some of the best coping skills for overcoming their difficulties. Yet still others were noticeably out of place and usually left the environment on their own if they were not fired first. Each of those people I met provided me with lessons for success that remain with me from some of my youngest years.

Take Charlie, he lived across the street from me in Detroit. As a young boy of 11 or 12 I would always see him working in his garage. Charlie despite any of his human failings was a good bicycle mechanic. As I got to know him I visited his garage that was cluttered with old bicycle parts from the floor to the ceiling, with only a narrow path to walk through to the back of the garage where in the clearing was his workbench. I even worked with him at his bicycle shop only to learn more about the mechanics of my own bicycle as I repaired other more sophisticated models. Charlie taught me how to use tools, properly maintain my bike and how

Where Do I Begin?

to upgrade the gear ratio of the front and rear sprockets. As a result of some of that instruction I always had the fastest coaster bike on the street and to this day I use his tips on aligning the wheels of my bike. But more than that he taught me how someone with simple skills could earn a living. Some of the first work I charged people money for was my ability to either repair or renovate a bicycle. I took a two dollar bicycle and restored it to like new condition years after production of the bicycle had ended. I earned twenty-five cents for the flat tire repairs done for others, but I sold the restored bicycle for the price of my first automobile. Even though Charlie is long gone now, at 65 years of age I still use some of the skills he taught me to maintain my bicycle.

I worked for my uncle for a short time after high school. He taught me how to braze carbide tips into cutting tools. It wasn't a sophisticated job, but you could earn a good living from it at that time. My uncle was frugal in the way he managed the business and enjoyed a middle class lifestyle as he worked year after year. The most significant lesson Uncle Carl taught me was when he asked me the question, what famous quotation do you remember? I promptly answered " To thine own self be true", from Shakespeare. Although I did not read a lot of Shakespeare, that one saying stayed with me from high school until now. What was the lesson? Well my answer so impressed my uncle that day as we worked there side by side considering the applications of such words as compared to their original intention, that I never forgot that moment and have gone back to it many times in search of a compass to guide my action.

Someone I met only once during a job interview that had advertised for shop foreman told me that despite my skill and understanding I did not have sufficient background for him to hire me as a shop foreman. He pointed out that even though I had accomplished much in my short work career the jobs I held never required me to carry the burden of other peoples' performance. I do not remember his name, but what he said was very instructive. From that time forward I looked for opportunities to work in team environments that eventually gave me opportunities to lead others in a larger effort. Leading an effort requires a different skill set than just getting the job done as an individual. Although I found I enjoyed the occasions I had to lead I also found that working as an individual was far more satisfying than working as a manager or shop foreman. That may say more about my personal preferences than it does about the value of the work.

Some years later I was working as a project manager responsible for providing plans and guidance for a shop foreman that unknown to me had constructed some tooling, critical to the company operation, that did not conform to plans I had prepared. For some reason he thought he had a better idea. Unfortunately for him he did not understand that I was able to examine the tooling and discover what he had done after he reported the tooling did not work. I politely asked him to redo the work as it was detailed and left out any argument. Shortly thereafter the plant manager summoned me to his office to discuss the required rework of the tools. I explained how I discovered the problem. He then asked me, could I get the work done without the shop foreman? Not knowing how much it would increase my workload I reluctantly said, yes. The shop foreman was gone that day and the work got done in his absence. The lesson learned was that circumstances have a way of testing your performance.

Let the experience you have accumulated help you make decisions that support your confidence. Be ready for the opportunity to always do more when you are called on by either an employer or a customer. The challenges you face present opportunity to learn and grow your talent for executing a plan. Nothing satisfies an employer or customer more than getting the job done. If you seek to be in business consider customers often.

Many businesses are compromised by customers that fail to make good on their part of the contract only because they know that a new business owner is vulnerable. Those same customers sound good to a person hungry for business, but when given an objective review will not pass the good customer test. As a new business person you will need to know, what are reasonable expectations of any customer? Use the reasonable rules of others offering a similar service as a starting point. Once you have established a positive cash flow you can refine your rules. Being objective and understanding what a variance from established rules might result in, must be foremost in your mind when customers ask for special consideration. Customers are like you and I, they want all the consideration they can get as long as they can get it. Some customers are more reasonable than others and those are the customers you want to cultivate. Reasonable customers expect to get what they pay for that is defined before the job begins and they also expect reasonable safe performance of any product that is a part of your service. This is not a difficult set of customer qualifications and if the customer wants to bargain for unreasonable terms do not settle for a bad customer. Move on and look for a better customer. Patience and persistence work while searching for customers just like they work for other aspects of your life.

Customers that are reasonable can become associates that you work with over a lifetime. Customers that take unfair advantage of you are not worth having as customers. A rule of thumb can be, do not make any extended agreements with people that haven't demonstrated they are worth your trust. There are few short cuts to being successful, so do not let your ambition to establish that first customer drive a costly agreement with any one customer.

As a small business person searching for a good customer I happened upon a business that from all outward appearances would seem to be a good candidate I reluctantly agreed to temporarily work with them so we could jointly pursue a larger customer. What I had overlooked was the size of our joint effort never could have handled even one order from the larger customer without overwhelming our capacity. After a week or so of discussion with the larger customer they told us we were not big enough to qualify at even an entry level. Fortunately it only cost me and my associate two weeks of time and few resources beyond that to get a final answer.

Several other bad starts taught me that finding a good match might not be as easy as I first thought. Instead I had to sift through a number of possibilities that never brought in any money before discovering several customers that provided me a good living over a seven to ten year period. I eventually went back to working as an employee for a large firm only because it seemed like a good idea at the time. I never thought I would be there very long,

Where Do I Begin?

but twenty-four years later I retired for the same reason, it seemed like a good idea at the time. Even while with my last employer I held nothing less than five different positions that served the same external customer.

The beginning is not necessarily the first job you hold. Beginning includes starting over and learning new things that work in different environments. As a designer I moved through a wide range of design environments. What was surprising was not finding other friends I knew making similar crossovers. People in the engineering environment tend to specialize staying with that specialty an entire lifetime. I enjoyed the variety and the challenges that the separate environments presented, but at the time found many of those opportunities when work I was more familiar with did not exist. Being open to new things will allow you to grow and prosper even when changing environments are challenging.

What is your favorite work environment? If it is working for yourself give yourself permission to work for someone else if only on a limited basis. If you are comfortable going to a single place every day, allow yourself to offer what you can do for a customer as a contracted service. When you do this you expand your opportunities for a job. Jobs will happen when you are open to different ways of selling the capability you and you alone possess.

If you have never held a sales job, consider getting one if for no other reason but getting in touch with the salesperson within yourself. If no one is willing to give someone with no experience an opportunity, hire yourself by having a garage sale. As a savvy shopper perhaps you know of several stores that need sales help. Avoid the get rich sales schemes that promise riches and a good life overnight. Stick with the conventional methods that offer you a first time opportunity, but still be creative.

If you have never provided a service or built a product look for entry levels jobs that can provide you with a new experience. Jobs will happen when you are looking for new opportunities. Buying and selling can be a job that never requires you produce anything, but a profit. Buying at a low price and selling at a slightly higher price will produce profit if done consistently over time. The benefit of selling without being the producer is avoiding the capital and inventory required to produce products for a customer. The disadvantage of not being the producer is being undercut by another sales source that gets a better price from the producer perhaps because they order larger quantities.

Regardless if you are a producer or simply a sales agent there is work to be done and those people that offer goods that people want at a price they are willing to pay will profit. A smaller market means the customer will probably be more selective, but many choices have been eliminated for the customer due to the business contraction. This should provide you with an opportunity to provide the customer more choice that is competitive with the remaining business that make up today's market.

When you need work it is difficult not to be constantly considering your own situation. To find the best opportunity for you it is important to change your focus to the customers that are still in today's market. Where are retailers doing best? Where are industrial firms doing best? Which professionals are doing best? The customers spending money everyday are seeking some of the choices they have lost and new offerings from someone just like you. Don't spend too much time standing in line with so many others for random job opportunities. Instead be out actively seeking customers that buy products and services one at a time from people just like you when given the right reason.

What reason makes the customer seek you out of all the rest? First and foremost, what product or service do you offer? Second, is the price competitive with the market and still include a profit to pay your wage? Third, where is your product available? Finally, how have you promoted the product or service you have to offer? Let's zero in on some of these details from an unemployed persons perspective.

Examine the past for things you may have produced either as part of jobs you have held or as a hobby. Now examine the media to identify what is selling today. Look at radio, newspapers, web portals, television and any mailers you receive. Try to find close if not identical matches between products and services you have been involved in producing and what is currently being advertised. Consider that the most popular products and services may have limited advertising, because they are in demand. Therefore something that is heavily advertized may be having a difficult time finding a customer. A large amount of advertisement is usually an indicator that you need to look elsewhere for a match between what you have to offer and the product being sold. Examples of this could range from the most popular cars to the most popular clothing. If something is in demand the producer is not likely to spend dollars advertising.

As an unemployed person that is looking for quick relief you must not only look for a popular product or service to associate yourself with, but you must be aware of other products that may compete with the item. Some of the best advertising for a popular product is driven by media discussion of a product that is not in the form of an advertisement. News coverage of people seeking a product in short supply around holidays usually shortens the supply even more than before such news. Is the competition filling a similar need at a better price? Only products and services that are in demand will have any potential to pay for themselves and a wage for you.

Even in a depressed economy when the product meets a need at a price the customer is willing to pay sales occur and jobs will happen as a result. It is worth taking some extra time to start with identifying the right product or service, because it makes all else easier by comparison. Having the right product or service makes it easier to identify the right price, or a price the customer is willing to pay that includes a margin sufficient to pay for your effort to sell it. Pricing power in a poor economy is usually limited, but backing the right product or service at least makes pricing power a variable.

Pricing can be enhanced by delivery service, maintenance service, warranties and personal coaching on use of the product. As an unemployed person without a lot of overhead or capital expense and no management team to limit the way you model a successful sale you must offer a better price. Do not sacrifice all profit and a living wage but be the competition other businesses with similar offerings envy. Even if the product or service you choose to sell has become a bit of a commodity with competitive biding, be among

Where Do I Begin?

the top three best values that others review. Consider that if you are successful in selling to one person you are very likely to need to improve or at least repeat the same experience for the customers that are sure to follow, so have a plan to repeat and improve customer experience.

Sometimes repeatability comes with the place you offer your product or service. Products offered on a web site can be a way of structuring the product information, the way to contact you, the way payment is made and the way a customer takes delivery. It can include promotions that are offered other places and link the customer to your web site. Doing business is not as expensive on the internet, and makes it is a great place for the unemployed to start.

If instead you have no understanding of technology and would prefer more one on one contact with customers, consider street vending and door to door sales. Street vending or even door to door sales may require a permit or license from the city, county or state. A short cut to finding your way through that maze would be to engage a local vendor and ask them what requirements they had to meet. If they say there were none, stop and go directly to the local city offices and ask the same questions.

Sometimes your product or service can be offered through a simple ad on a bulletin board at a friends business or a local grocery store that allows public postings. Handbills are another way to distribute your information to a large neighborhood. Some companies for a very small piece cost will distribute your offering among several zip codes in your neighborhood. If you have carefully selected the product or service and followed it with competitive pricing your offering can be in the mail box of thousands of neighbors in a couple of weeks or less.

Finally consider how you will promote your offer. So many discounts are offered by so many businesses that discounts at some point do not have the impact you might hope. Instead consider promotions that focus on other aspects of the sale. Free delivery, fast delivery and a free gift to complement the product or service you offer are all possible promotions. Keep in mind that the promotion needs to be something that not only attracts the first

Where Do I Begin?

sale, but repeated sales to the same person. Sometimes twenty percent or less of the customers will provide you with eighty percent or more of your business.

As I sit contemplating what to say next the latest statistics for unemployment are being discussed by newscasters. The numbers are a tsunami of bad news that may still get worse. We need to stay in touch with the reality of our situation while not to interrupting our focus on places to start over. Seeking opportunities for work in places where work is needed and first likely to occur after a recession is important in improving the odds that a job or a customer will be available for you.

The old way of looking for work was to just apply at advertised firms or perhaps at those businesses nearest your home. I would suggest a new way to begin your job search is with the most likely businesses or customers that are currently profiting despite the downturn in the economy. Regardless of some of the staggering numbers more than 80 percent of the workforce in America is still working and producing. The economy is currently still shrinking, but that means new ideas that grow jobs and provide work for you and others is still not getting traction. I would contend that there is greater opportunity for new business with low capital requirements and an ability to deliver small quantities. Customers are buying, but in smaller quantities and spreading there limited funds over a wider range of products.

You can offer customers new ways to spend their savings or income. This book will publish after the Christmas Holiday season of 2009 so seasonal opportunities will be behind you as you read this book. However opportunities going into 2010 are endless. How can I possibly say that considering that layoffs from seasonal hiring are likely to occur? Well most retailers and you may count yourself among the retailers are working six to twelve months ahead of any season. For an unemployed person looking for a job consider those jobs available three to six months from now, because it will take you several weeks or months to ready the product or service that you will offer a customer or employer.

If you seem to be in a cycle of one short term job after another consider it a positive, because you are ahead of the person

Where Do I Begin?

that is consistently unemployed. In 2010 business is not expected to grow at much more than two percent. The significant thing about that number is that it has been taking business growth of three to four percent to create jobs and for the unemployment numbers to begin to recede. That is a very general statement that may or may not have any relevance to you and your situation. I say that because I know that when it comes to creating work and some specific job no source has been more successful at creating jobs than small business. If you begin to think of yourself as a new small business venture the odds of finding work or even a job are far better than any of the statistics that are being generated in an effort to communicate the plight of people today.

By thinking of yourself as a business person first and as an employee second you improve your odds of finding either a customer or an employer. If you only think of yourself as an employee you reduce your chance of finding work by at least two thirds by my convoluted calculation. Remember you do not need a place of business to be in business in today's world. You only need to establish a positive cash flow that is consistent and can be sustained over time. You may be holding garage sales, buying and selling items online, doing odd jobs in the neighborhood you live in, or selling a product or service on a limited basis. Any one of these things or any combination of them can be your way to succeed.

In the beginning start with you and everything that defines you to discover what you can produce for someone. Establish a competitive price for your product or service, based on what potential customers are currently paying for similar products or services. Decide where you will establish contact with customers and potential employers. Will you advertise in the newspaper, through the mail, over the telephone, at a store front or online using a web site? Finally consider how you will promote your product or service in a way that will not only capture a first time buyer, but encourage customers to return many times over.

Chapter 3

Who is in Charge?

Yes it is you. There may be a lot of things you do not have control over, asserting yourself is not in that category. You are in charge of your vision for the future and the effort you are willing to make it happen. Yes there are obstacles and there always are if you are trying to do something. The path of many is to hesitate and go slow. It is important that you choose to do something that will make a difference to build the confidence that will sustain you through any period of unemployment.

Consider accomplishment and just getting things done as a way of life. If you lack energy, if you lack motivation, if you lack a plan and yes if you lack any history of accomplishment do not consider yourself a lost cause or without hope. You will need to start by determining that you are still in charge of making things happen for yourself. Thinking quietly to yourself "I am in charge" and repeating that thought throughout the day is a way to reinforce what may not have been obvious to you. Immediately after thinking "I am in charge" do something that has been undone and needs doing. That something can be as simple as cleaning your living space or as organized as preparing a room for paint.

If you are thinking, what does this have to do with getting a job? When you lost a job either yesterday or a year ago, it was a time when you lost control of your schedule or were given total control of your schedule. How did you view the event? Were you feeling a bit lost or were you now free to pursue a vision that you were restrained from pursuing the day before you lost your job? Most people would say they were a bit lost. The way to turn that feeling around even a year or more after you lost your job is by taking control of your life a little at a time until you have established some history of accomplishment that you can use as encouragement for doing more. Starting with what seems like small and insignificant tasks is a way of establishing early success instead of pursuing objectives with a high risk. Nothing will sustain and motivate you more than success over time. The high risk opportunities will always be there for you in the future, but what you need after a big loss is some rebuilding of both your confidence and history of success. Try to include in that list of things to do, things that will make you a healthier person. Eating and exercising in appropriate amounts will help move you along a path that sustains you during more difficult times. Like other things you do eating and exercising routines are habits that need to be established if they are to provide you with benefits.

Taking control of your life is different for everyone, but similar in some basic ways. First understand that anyone can loose control of events in their life. How a person responds to the loss of control is where the differences become noticeable. At one end of the scale people are devastated and their life seems to spiral out of control and at the other end of the scale life is interrupted, but the person seems to flourish and go on to a better life. Being in charge of your life has as much to do with avoiding self destructive behavior as does taking positive steps following a disaster. If the positive steps you take in response to a setback are countered by self destructive behavior at best progress is cancelled out at worst you may continue to loose control going forward.

I like so many people have been setback either through my own doing or through events I had little or virtually no control over. Fortunately I have recovered from those and that learning process over the years has helped me recover from setbacks that occur as life happens. Here are some of the things I have learned. First doing nothing is not a good response, because you tend to loose ground despite avoiding any self destructive behavior. If the event is a pending event, acting before the event may help you avoid a more severe loss. When you ask for help ask people that can make a difference. Family members, employers and friends may be able to give you some short term relief. Finally and the most important thing to do is take regular positive steps to reclaim control over your life.

When you are going through an out control event positive changes do not seem to happen quickly enough. Being patient and persistent in your application of positive action is critical to securing a measure of change that satisfies your need to see progress. Even

Who is in Charge?

when additional setbacks occur during your recovery process the progress you have made in the past will help sustain continuing efforts in a positive direction. The speed of positive changes can be improved by putting in place as many seeds for positive change as possible. When you are unemployed do something everyday that makes you more qualified for a job or more familiar with the business and customers you want to serve. When you meet with employers share the daily efforts you make to succeed. When you excite someone else about what you are doing they may look for ways to help without you asking for assistance. They may share your positive thinking and energetic effort with others you don't know that may in turn want to get involved with your effort. A famous car salesman Joe Gerard said, "each person knows about 250 people", in his book "How to Sell Anybody Any Thing". The significance of that is that your conversations with friends can travel far and fast if the conversation impresses the person you speak with in a positive way.

No matter where you start the choices you make or neglect to make will propel you toward a destination that is unknown. Improving the odds that objectives and goals you set get done along the path you follow depends on you taking control over what you say and do everyday. Like it or not you have a part to play in controlling that next opportunity. A funny thing happened to me when I was young and on the way home after I was hired by a large manufacturing company following a rather difficult interview. Instead of rejoicing that I was given an opportunity to work for a large and stable company that is in business to this day I continued down the road to a much smaller company and accepted a job with them. The next day I called the large company and informed them I would not be reporting to work. Why given those choices would I drop the first more capable employer for a second small business? As I sat through the interview of the first larger company all that stood out in the conversation was their emphasis on how restrictive and limiting the work would be from the first day and for some time in the future. The second employer emphasized their need for someone that could contribute in as many ways as possible, and how they would expand my opportunity to do new things as I demonstrated an ability to get the job done. The decision for me

Who is in Charge?

was a "no brainer". I started the next day and enjoyed every day I worked there despite a 12 hour a day schedule 7 days a week for some time to come. I have no doubt looking back on that decision that I did the right thing. If I had not had a choice between two jobs I may have taken the first offer and then had a lot of motivation to keep looking afterwards. Even while working at the more favored job I continued to pursue better opportunities until being hired by a new company only several months later. The new company had a four year training program I would qualify for several months after being hired.

There are always opportunities during good times, but discovering the opportunities during a recession requires you to work harder at improving the odds of getting a job by being available for more kinds of work than just what is most familiar. The current recession is a very difficult period as compared to all others. It is also different given our place in history. This can be a time when you discover great opportunities that will in turn make some of the bad experiences you may have had easier to put behind you.

During the recession of the early seventies I was working as a contract designer off and on. Work even on a contract basis became difficult to find regularly. I had heard about training programs being run by private schools and community colleges sponsored by the federal government. I considered trying to get a teaching position with one of them for a short period of time to help pay my bills. Was I qualified? Well I would leave that determination to those people that had the job of considering my application. I visited several of the schools in the Detroit area and came across a small school in Detroit. The school was in an old building on Grand River Avenue and only a half hour drive from my home. The school was organized to train people for several engineering disciplines and the job I was given was to instruct the students how to read and develop mechanical drawings.

Like some new ventures this one was off to a rocky start, the class was comprised of post high school men and women that were struggling with the second or third instructor to run the class within the last few months. It was reasonable for them to question the schools new choice of instructors. This was my first teaching assignment and their first opportunity to learn something that may result in employment. Approximately two thirds or more were unemployed and trying to get that measure of skill that may lead to a job. It seems a bit ironic my being rescued from unemployment by a job that required me to teach other people skills that could in turn rescue them from unemployment. Some of these people were chronically unemployed, that is to say they were unemployed for over a year or more with few if any job prospects.

At first I used the text book the school provided, but soon discovered this was not going to give the students what they needed to satisfy any of the employers I had come across in the past. So in an attempt to not only gain control of the class but deliver training that could be translated into a job I told the management they would need to give me a bit more flexibility to structure a program that could satisfy the students needs and make running a class with multiple disciplines more manageable from a instructors' point of view.

The next day I announced that the text book assignments would be minimal and we would regard the text as a reference while we explored developing a portfolio of drawings for each individual that would be aligned with the program that was directly related to the school program they signed up for weeks or months ago. The class was more manageable going forward and once people began to see what they were able to produce they worked harder and longer in an effort to produce a portfolio that would demonstrate their competence and progress to the next prospective employer. At the end of approximately nine months the entire class was invited to visit with a prospective employer that had visited the school. Although many students had already secured work, many more were invited to work with this new employer.

I left shortly after that to return to contracting design work, but later got a job with a large company providing remedial training for long time employees that needed to improve their skills. I never would have predicted that sequence of job opportunities that occurred just when few jobs were available and my need for a job was great. The patience and persistence I needed to work through

Who is in Charge?

those somewhat trying times reinforced for me that small but positive steps can overcome obstacles that occur as a part of any new adventure. Certainly the jobs that came about for many people in that class demonstrated how a focused effort and some novel approaches to preparing for a job can change lives.

If the future is so unpredictable how can someone say that getting skills or an education will change the plight of the jobless? It is because new jobs and jobs that return during every business cycle require some level of skill and understanding of fundamentals. The new jobs always apply some of the old skills in new ways, but the old jobs that return usually require more understanding of the latest products and technology. One of the best examples of new jobs that require old skills could be those machinists that once made car parts and now make parts for windmills that generate electricity. An example of old jobs requiring more understanding would include auto mechanics. Auto mechanics in 1960 did not need any skill or understanding of computer modules that control many functions of the automobile today. As an auto mechanic today skill and understanding of computer modules is a part of diagnostics for many problems that affect virtually all vehicles today.

You are in charge of making a plan that will include training and education that you need to support any objectives or goals you determine fit your vision of the future. An unpredictable future still requires your plan for action that will either prepare you for new job opportunities or help you keep pace with changes that impact jobs that are needed even in a bad economy. Standing still or opting to do nothing in a difficult job market translates into falling behind the competition for the same work by other people. Some of the best paying jobs are skilled or semiskilled work. So do not overlook jobs that require training not a college degree. Many semiskilled jobs are available throughout the country making the opportunity for work more likely.

Just as we hear that the economy is turning around more news today that the 98 banks have failed as of October 2, 2009 http://www.fdic.gov/index.html. On October 9, 2009 vacancy rates of commercial property is at a 17 year low. That news is not surprising when the employment numbers are at a 26 year low.

Who is in Charge?

Yet there are still new opportunities to work make money and yes even get a job. Some opportunities are better than others and some opportunities require a fair amount of capital and risk. Consider someone that is not unemployed, but has a business that is under stress. A few situations I have observed lately include business people that are deferring tax payments, selling assets, revising customer contracts to continue to stay in business. These business people even though not technically unemployed have negative cash flow businesses and are adjusting their debt payments to continue to stay in business as they look for new opportunities to improve their income revenue. What separates them from people that go out of business?

For some of these people this is a way of life. Juggling income and bills due has been a problem from the first day they did business and today is just another day. Unfortunately many are finding out due to the depth and breath of this recession that they need something more than a few deferred payments to stay in business. A neighbor of mine has added stone work to his roofing business. He has had to invest considerable effort and capital to include this to his offering, but over several months he seems to have prospered as a result of his efforts. A neighborhood builder although deferring tax payments on existing properties is continuing to build new dwellings and closing sales on existing properties in the neighborhood. A local realtor that manages commercial properties has had to subdivide properties into smaller parcels and offer month to month leases to find businesses willing to locate on his properties.

What does this have to do with unemployment and finding a job? Well you might remember I asked you consider self employment as well as just applying for a job. Regardless of the strain that this economy has put on employees and employers alike self employment is still another opportunity to find work. It may require you to be a bit more careful with your expenses, but it still offers opportunity to work at something more challenging as well as more profitable over time. Being in business can be simple if your business model is a simple one, but if your vision of business

Who is in Charge?

requires combining multiple skills to deliver your product or service it will take more care and planning before you take action. If we were looking for a job creating machine sold at a large retail outlet, what would it look like? It would be a package that contained instructions that would allow any individual with initiative, patience and persistence to put together a small business from scratch. Small business is an opportunity that the individual has to take charge of their life creating a living wage from work they can do in an environment that has lost other small businesses due to an economic downturn. It is not the last opportunity to get work in that same environment, because that is where the government usually steps in to provide make work projects. All honest work is legitimate, but reliance on the government for a job should be our last option.

Work that depends on private sector customers has been the way our nation has become the biggest economy in the world regardless of the size of our population. The beauty of small business depending on private sector customers is that these customers exist everywhere from border to border. Government programs that provide work are limited in more ways than one. Before you consider what the government has to offer stop to consider what you have to offer those private sector customers and how they might be willing to pay you for the work you are willing to do today.

As the person in charge of what you do next, choose to do something that will make you a job creator even if the only job you provide is one for yourself. You may start as fractional small business or micro business, until your finances are more stable. If all you provide is supplemental income for yourself now it may become full time employment later. Starting small is what small business is all about. Keep it simple, and make it cash flow positive at some point. Examine what other people have done to save time and money. Learn to satisfy the demands of the customers you have identified. You will always have critics of any effort, but if you satisfy several customers repeatedly it is an indication that you have put together a winning combination that can prosper over time. Be careful not to loose your way as you achieve a measure of success.

Who is in Charge?

If you are detoured for any reason let the customer show you the way back to prosperity.

Detours happen for a reason. Did you spend to much, or not enough? Are you considering a plan to get where you want to be over some period of time, or are you just letting other people determine your fate? In my early years I had a tendency to step into some pretty big potholes that would take long periods of recovery and keep me from enjoying my prosperity. Today I make fewer mistakes and recover much more quickly. I have also learned to savor everyday even during those times when I am recovering from a detour. Staying optimistic helps weather those periods of recovery, because they are rarely predictable. Stay in charge of what you do next to the extent it depends on what you can do. The effort to stay on course with your plan is never wasted, because it will serve to either get you where you want to be or teach you a lesson you may never forget.

Some of the best decisions I have made were made after sustaining significant losses. Deciding not to let setbacks allow an out of control situation to persist limits losses and prepares you to engage the next opportunity to reclaim losses sustained. Taking control of your life not only involves making decisions and executing a plan to get things done it requires resilience when you sustain setbacks. Bouncing back is essential to success, because sustaining losses along the way is just a normal part of the process. Countless successful people have had large setbacks throughout their history, but they are resilient and comeback quickly after any sustained loss. Sometimes you need to take a short break from the activity that went wrong, but sooner or later you need to confront any fear you may have and try again. Maybe you got sloppy and let too much risk creep into the operation. Perhaps there are new elements that did not get considered when you made a decision that led to a loss. Whatever it is that went wrong you need to consider how you contributed to the poor decision for action before trying to succeed again.

After being away from skydiving for a while I went back and on my first jump I had a delayed opening of my parachute that required me to deploy my reserve parachute. Needless to say I was

Who is in Charge?

more than a little upset and puzzled how this could happen. After consulting with a master rigger at the jump center he asked me to pack my chute in his presence. As I got about 25% complete he stopped me and pointed to the way I was packing the lines. He said I was packing in a way that could easily delay an opening or even prevent a complete opening in some instances. I was relieved that I was making such a glaring error that could easily be corrected. My next parachute jump was without incident and I went on to complete about 60 jumps before deciding not to continue the sport. Had I ignored finding a solution to that setback I may have quit much earlier and had doubts about what went wrong without ever knowing.

Some years later as a young designer I was working with an older project engineer that had me working on a special machine that required adding some counterbalance components to the design. Despite my best calculations a single variable within the production process that I had overlooked while the machine ran made the estimates of the counterbalance wrong. Not realizing this I had the machine built as designed. When the machine was started up the counterbalance units almost seemed useless as the machine cycled out of control. I was so upset I was ready to throw up my hands and leave the problem to someone else, but the steady hand of the project engineer quickly had me double my effort to review the production process. As I went back and took a second look it was apparent what I had missed. With only the addition of one extra counterbalance the special purpose machine worked just as intended. Without that coaching I would have walked away sacrificing a well paying job for what in the end was a simple correction.

When you set out to succeed in business or at a job, the way you make decisions elsewhere in your life will surely influence your decisions, actions, resilience, patience and persistence you afford yourself and others. Bouncing back from mistakes and taking advice from others at a time when all you want to do is crawl in bed and cover your head with a blanket can be the only action that keeps you from loosing control.

Who is in Charge?

Are you ready to take charge in your life? If you are unemployed it is a good time to start, because there probably isn't anyone challenging you for that job. As a matter of fact others may have put some distance between you and them, because they are uncomfortable talking about what is going on in your life at this time. Perhaps your plight is a bit frightening to others and they just don't want to be reminded of how it might impact them if they lost their job. Whatever your circumstance it can be improved by you taking control over the smallest of decisions and striving for an improvement in your situation.

Depending on your personality you will be inclined to start gaining control in different ways. Some people like to take bold steps that advance their objectives and goals. Others are less adventurous and are satisfied with small gains. Try to minimize the risk when you consider your next action big or small. Managing risk is the easiest way to make incremental gains over time. Using low risk opportunities to make both bold moves and small gains leads to building confidence. Aren't bold moves more risky? Yes, but the odds of failure rise exponentially when bold moves are taken at the wrong time. The difference between big and small moves should not be your ability to loose money, but timing larger moves for times that hold least risk. Small moves that use careful timing can accumulate money for large moves in the future. If you are successful, a component of that success is timing the things you do to achieve gains to a narrow timetable that reduces your risk of failure.

Once you understand that being successful in part depends on limiting your risk you can begin to identify the signposts that tell you when risk is low. Watch how people move as a herd and do your best to make moves ahead of the herd instead of after the herd moves based on fundamental reasons for doing anything. As an example let us look at the type of events that move people like a herd to take action. When bad weather approaches where you live do you consider staying in place or getting out of harms way? Do you monitor the local, national and world news to be aware of events that may require your involvement to move ahead of others to take advantage of opportunities to either profit or avoid loss?

Who is in Charge?

People that make decisions without first gaining a perspective that identifies the level of risk will put them at risk of loss for small and large decisions. If you are not sure what the risk is ask others how they arrive at their conclusions. People that have thought long and hard about what creates risk are not hesitant to share that with you. Do not make your decision based on one opinion, ask other people or look for published opinions on the subject by professionals that follow the subject of interest.

Large and small expenses devoted to either getting a job or getting customers for a small business can be spent on a low risk basis. If the reason for spending the money seems too good to be true ask for a second opinion. As you spend money evaluate the benefits that you expect to receive against the benefits you actually receive. Include some analysis before and after decisions to reduce the risk of making a faulty decision that cost money, time and energy. You may not avoid all risk, but minimizing risk improves the odds of profiting from decisions everyday.

Find ways of measuring the risk of decisions before you make them in a world that cost real money and resources. Some people call this technical analysis. Try to discover patterns that are predictable to some degree. Patterns that predict direction are a good way to minimize risk when the direction of your decisions is not clear. Can you also determine the times of day that minimize risk. Finally try to determine what the level of support or resistance is present for the direction you would take. Maximizing support and minimizing resistance means your direction has less risk. These methods work for minimizing risk on a diverse group of decisions. Risk assessment can be valuable in preserving limited resources when you are unemployed or just trying to improve your financial condition going forward.

Specific risk reducing techniques that can be generally applied would include, but are not limited to doing analysis and making decisions when you are well rested, gathering several opinions to consider, and identifying the path of least resistance. Here is how you apply those techniques in your search for a customer or a job. Analysis and decisions on what your plan for tomorrow is should happen in the early evening hours. Gathering

Who is in Charge?

opinions can be done in a library setting or over the telephone likewise in the early evening hours. Finally identifying the path of least resistance as a direction to take is only valid if it includes avoiding illegal and immoral behavior. When people are desperate to secure employment or just enough money to pay their bills the temptation to do the wrong thing is great. Do not give into these fatal errors of judgment. They tend to set you up for life long setbacks.

Taking charge of what you do to either compete for one of the few jobs available or create one for yourself is essential. You are not obligated to ask anyone for permission to take charge of your life. Everyone may have limitations they work within, but when it comes to the everyday routine that will build better habits and connect you with people that may become customers or employers you have full control. Most people are bored by the tedious task of building good habits. Usually people only applaud larger achievements and you are left to praise yourself for the small efforts that make a difference over time. It might be what you save by making your own coffee everyday versus going to a restaurant for coffee, or perhaps keeping track of the price of groceries from one store to another. The same way these small opportunities escape our observation is the same way that details important to a customer are ignored by the producer of a product or service. Some of the wealthiest and most successful people are very detail oriented. You do not need to be excessive compulsive about detail, but you do need to appreciate that customers do observe details and even compare identical products for flaws between them. A process that is stable and produces consistently superior products or services is usually rewarded.

If news reports are true and there are six people for every job available with an unemployment rate at 9.8% in October of 2009, you will need to do a lot of thinking about how you will compete in the marketplace. If 50% to 80% of all new jobs are created by small business it is reasonable to consider that you have a better chance of creating your own job than you have of standing in line with thousands of people waiting for someone to create a job just for you with the unemployment rate continuing to rise. As a

Who is in Charge?

one person low budget small business venture you do have some limitations, but likewise you have some great advantages that other larger businesses do not have, because of their size. You only need to make enough money to cover expenses for one person and a living wage. The products and services you offer can be as diverse as need be or focused on a single high margin item. When you are in charge all the options are available.

As a micro business it does not take a lot of business to keep doing business. It can be a part-time business until you have more customers. Bookkeeping and tax claims are fairly simple as an unincorporated business. The customer of the small business will consider the micro business on a word of mouth reference or on a well placed advertisement. Some fairly large companies started out as a micro business. Focus on making a living day to day by satisfying each customer and allowing for a wage and a profit. If adding a profit to your expenses and wage are difficult to negotiate with a customer consider a promotion in exchange for the profit on some sales and not on others. Some customers may be willing to promote your business to reduce the price they pay. As a micro business you are in charge of all of the business decisions that need to be made to convince that next customer to choose you over the next business.

What are the first and most difficult elements of business to control? Expectations are the most difficult to control, because they are different for every customer. Customer expectations that need to be high on the list of business priorities include quality, safety and price. Certainly other things like availability, quick delivery and other elements are important, but if you fall short on quality, safety or price a customer may never consider availability or quick delivery.

A rather good customer had called me back to review a piece of work I provided, to my surprise it was full of errors I could not deny existed. It happened to be a busy time and the business associate that did the work was an old friend. He always seemed competent in other instances and I was shocked that he had let me down in this way. I called him up and explained the situation and unfortunately he determined he was too busy to make the corrections immediately. I painstakingly went through each element of the work correcting it before returning to the customer. The customer was very disappointed in the delay and the number of errors that needed correction and left the impression it was the last time I would see him. I did get limited work from him in the future, but only a fraction of what I received before this one incident. This was a costly customer complaint. I had to decide to control the quality much more closely going forward and avoid any overload that would not permit scrutiny of what was delivered to the customer. I never did use my friend on a contract basis again for any work. From that day forward I was concerned with quality more than most of my customers. As a micro business or a small business quality along with many other customer expectations will depend on the owner to control.

If you are not inclined to take control of your life in any one of many ways you may likewise find it difficult to either get a job or start a business. Being in charge is important, but staying in charge is more important. Other people can be assigned tasks and responsibility, but as an employee or as an owner you always must take charge where it is appropriate. As an employee I always had to build safeguards into my work processes, because most of what people requested was on a moments notice or at the very least with a early deadline. Anytime you add speed to what you do you add risk of error, fortunately in my later years I usually had a rather detailed manager that would backstop my error checking. It would always annoy me if he was able to find something, but I knew he was right and I would redouble my efforts to check my work. Certainly his calm and understanding approach made me work harder the next time, and it certainly tempered my remarks about others errors that I discovered. When you work alone as a contract service you do not usually have that consideration by customers that may only have a single order or two for you to fill.

If being in charge or taking control of your life seems like an odd consideration of someone that is unemployed or without customers consider an employee or business person that does not feel they are in charge. That employee would be very unsure about every decision they made and would require constant coaching and supervision. The business person that lacks a sense of being in charge would probably lack confidence to pitch their product or service. How would a customer treat a business person that lacked confidence in what they had to offer? As a customer myself I would probably seek another sales person or have more questions about the product than ever. Successful employees and business people alike are confident and almost in charge to a fault.

If you lack confidence and a measure of being in control start improvement in your personal life, because you may be more familiar with the actions that are out of control. Pick something that would be improved by increased control. Consider something like your level of activity or your eating habits. I say activity to avoid that word that some people dread, exercise. I say activity to purposely include all things you do that contribute to the exercise you need.

If you find that you have become more sedentary due to unemployment take action to correct that situation. Make a list of places to go if only to window shop or get a breath of fresh air. Increase that list every day until your physical activity is measurably more than what it was a month after you began the effort. If you do that you will have taken control and will be in charge of something.

If your eating habits are not what they should be work on improving one meal at a time. When you find a nourishing set of items you can alternate at breakfast and develop a routine focus on lunch alternatives with that in place move to choices that make good choices for dinner. A month after you have reworked breakfast, lunch and dinner compare the scale reading from that first day and measure your success. Once again you are in charge and in control of something real.

Both of those examples were very simple approaches to better health and certainly if you need more support include a support group of your choice. The bottom line is if you do something you gain control. Likewise with your search for work and a job or a business if you do something even something small you begin to gain control.

Who is in Charge?

When I first kicked around the idea of going into business while unemployed I did not have any understanding of where to begin. First I asked an uncle of mine that was an accountant, how to setup my bookkeeping? Then I looked around for a building that I could use as an office. I needed a month to month rent, because I was not interested in a long lease. Next I negotiated for some equipment that would give my work a professional look. Finally I built some of the office furniture myself and a sign for the building. The total investment was under five hundred dollars. Today although I am retired I have found much less expensive ways to generate income. That first experience was well worth the effort because the first contract not only paid me a wage it covered the entire five hundred dollars. I used that business to generate income over a seven to ten year period. It really is surprising what you can do if you take control of the events in your life.

I did all of that before the personal computer and the internet existed. The opportunity to work and generate income today is so much improved by the technology that exist today that it might be one of the first places you have gone to find work. If it has not been a fruitful experience you may have just approached the medium as a consumer instead of a producer. Instead of looking for entertainment on the internet look for information that can improve your income. Some websites will let you sell items just as if you have set up a garage sale. Some websites will let you listen and watch experts explain business and give a wide range of opinions on how to invest the least of funds at no cost to you. Unemployed people need to shift from consuming to production. Anyone can make production their predominant use of the internet. Social networking can be helpful but there are ways to make a lot of money that may not require communicating with any person directly. As odd as that may seem it is more possible today than ever before to find a niche business that can satisfy customers around the world without direct customer contact. I buy and sell to people from all parts of the world and I never meet a one directly. Did I mention the marketplace was open 24 hours a day and as much as seven days a week 365 days a year? If all you want to work is 40 hours a week you will need to decide when during that range you are available. The approach to work today must include using technology if you want more opportunity and more flexibility in your work schedule. Limit using the internet for entertainment or to consume goods. Create an action plan that promotes a productive use of the internet. Get control of what you do and when you do it.

What you choose to do daily becomes the habit that will either support you or drain you of your resources. Some people do not see the connection between good habits and prosperity. A friend of mind who will remain nameless has some bad habits that are costing him hundreds of dollars per month and he strikes me as a pretty average person in so many other ways. The one habit he has that has burdened him for years is clutter. He may be described as a "hoarder" or someone that cannot seem to control his compulsion to accumulate things. He some time ago became unemployed and was asking for ideas on ways to balance his bills against his cash available. His home is by his account filled wall to wall with things. He also pays for two storage sheds monthly for approximately three hundred dollars per month. When I suggested he spend a weekend clearing the sheds and saving the rent he said he has no where to put the items. Come to find out much of what fills the sheds his home and even his van are marginally valued items. As much as hoarding may be an illness it is a bad habit that people can address one step at a time. He has found work recently but is still unable to pay all his bills on time in part because he is still burdened by the rental of his storage sheds.

Over a year ago I had a bad habit of eating too much on a regular schedule. I was sixty pounds overweight and had trouble tying my own shoes. Since then I got help and gained the control I needed to loose the weight, and now I am much more energetic and healthy as a result. If only it were that easy. It was not easy, but it was much easier than I had thought it would be when I first decided to address the problem.

When your habits threaten either your health or your ability to function while you are unemployed make an effort to get help to get them under control. Being in charge of how you operate from day to day is a foundation of any future you may envision for yourself. It may save your life, your savings and earn you a job going forward. Personal bad habits if they are noticeable to the

Who is in Charge?

casual observer will be obvious to the job interviewer or a potential customer. Employers are cautious, because of an uncertain future. Likewise with all the products to pick from customers are sensitive to the business person involved in their shopping experience.

Being in charge of personal habits despite unemployment will usually give you confidence. So if you need to boost your confidence on any given day try taking charge of even the smallest thing in your life that day. One of the habits I have worked to change is that of inactivity. I find it very easy to sit around and just let the world go by as I just observe. As a consequence I would get behind on some of the things that need doing. To combat that habit I have identified many small and limited tasks that I can work on at a moments notice to move me toward completion of larger goals. A period of inactivity for more than fifteen minutes during any day will trigger doing these tasks that always boost my confidence.

Some people make themselves busy as a way to avoid doing things that need to be done. Using deadlines to trigger your doing planned tasks to accomplish goals can be helpful. Years ago I committed to going back to college and completing requirements needed to receive my bachelor degree. Well like so many people I got busy doing other things, but I had set a deadline to make a commitment. The day of the deadline I was in the middle of painting the exterior of my house when it occurred to me that time had run out. I had plenty of reasons not to interrupt what I was doing that day, but I did and today I have my degree. Once again it wasn't that easy. There were many days I thought to myself why am I putting myself through this at this time in my life. I did not go back to college until I was 55 and finally completed requirements when I was 57. It surprised me and probably many others. If you tend to make yourself busy to avoid keeping commitments try setting some deadlines on your commitments. Deadlines will require you to consider that commitment and give you another opportunity to make good on plans you previously made.

If you are considering small business as an employment option you need to develop routines that make you available for doing business during business hours. Unemployment has a way of interrupting established routines and limiting your availability. Even if your schedule was an evening or night shift, regroup and establish a daytime routine or a routine that supports talking to business people during the day. Purchasing agents and personnel departments are available during daylight hours, as are most customers.

You know you are in charge when you can provide some forecast of the day. You may not be able to predict the events as much as you are able to predict the trend. As you continue to add positive accomplishments to the list of things completed during any given day it will signal that the trend is positive. That positive trend is what you should be working to achieve every day to build routines that support opportunity. Success is not usually a part of a day that has a negative trend. Strive to make as many days trend positive as is possible. It is on those days that have a positive trend that you will find a job or find a customer. The job opportunity or customer may come in the form of a challenge to get something done that has been undone for some time. I had contacted a carpenter to install crown mouldings in my family room. When we discussed the work that needed to be done and the cost he said if I was willing to serve as his helper and hold the other end of the mouldings as he aligned them for installation I could save the cost of his hiring a helper. Knowing I would probably be under his feet all day any way I agreed to be that extra set of hands he needed. The job was expedited and I got to learn some valuable lessons about what it actually took to do that particular job, and I saved some money over the next few days.

One of the first things that a person misses when they become unemployed is predictability of their day. So as you reestablish a routine and a positive trend for days that you are not formally employed you will loose that sense of loss. How can that improved sense of control contribute to the opportunities for work and employment? If the new routines you establish include activity that will either seek customers or employers you are on the right track. It is not enough to have a good day and expect work to come your way. You must actively seek work as part of your daily routine. It can be a difficult given the current state of our economy.

Who is in Charge?

When unemployment was down around four percent you did not need to be particularly patient or persistent to obtain work. Now with unemployment at levels about to top ten percent, a rate not seen in twenty five years, work is scarce. The most difficult experiences are those that make it seem like getting a job would be like winning a lottery. Standing in long lines with hundreds or even thousands of people that are showing up to a publicized job fair is not that uncommon. Your time is probably better spent looking for that job that is not advertised.

Talk to friends and keep in touch with your community. The events that are attended by the eighty to ninety percent of people that still have jobs is where you will find opportunity for work without standing in line. Identify the businesses in your community that continue to have business despite the economy. Recently I have noticed a hot dog vendor that moves from business to business making short term agreements with the businesses to either attract traffic or to share his profit with the local business. He has created work where traffic exists. I have seen him at gas stations and out in the street in front of the county court house. Not everybody can be a hot dog vendor, but everyone can be more creative about how they seek work.

Taking charge of your job search in a creative way may improve the experience and the results. Start with determining the range of work you will be willing to do in very specific terms. When you define the work it makes it much easier to determine where someone would look for people that do that kind of work. A well defined service or product is much easier to price in a competitive way. Finally decide on how you can best promote the work you can do for others.

Specialists are important and having a special skill will limit your competition. Special skills tell an employer or a customer that you have taken the time to learn details about a particular subject that perhaps ensures a greater level of quality and safety in the product or service you provide. When the overall market for work collapses as it has and your skills are not in demand they still have a value. Those same skills depended on certain fundamental learning traits that you can apply to a new skill. Small business values people that have multiple skills to offer. During the recession of the 1980's I had multiple skills. To my surprise one of the employers was rather dismissive of the skills that took nearly twenty years to cultivate instead they were interested in what I did as a hobby in the last six years. It was that hobby that got me that job. Over the next five years my work centered more and more on what I had done as a hobby. When I finally departed thinking I was headed to a more conventional environment nothing could be farther from the truth.

My next job as a designer with a large company started out quite average and comfortable. After being there for a little over a year I was asked to do a multitude of other things, because of my diverse background. Several years before retirement I was called on to use skills I developed as a hobby twenty years earlier to automate our reporting process.

Today most people at large companies that may have done one thing for many years are routinely asked to constantly do new things. This does not mean always doing something different, but doing multiple things daily. Similar to how small business has always worked. Small business is an excellent training ground for someone hoping to make a difference at a large company. As an unemployed person you need to assemble all that you are as an offering. You may have accumulated a lot of experience in an area of work that is out of demand today, but what were the skills or habits that made you do that job well? Are you a detailed person? Are you a person that likes to arrive on time? Are you a person that is good with customers? Do you enjoy doing many different tasks as part of your daily work? Do you have an activity that you are passionate about that requires special skills? You need to ask yourself all of these questions and more to get a better idea of how others see you. If you reveal some not so pretty parts of what makes you who you are take charge of correcting the shortcomings. An employer may ask if you have ever overcome any difficult problems just to determine if you are blind to your own faults or have any coping skills. Personal stories of how you have overcome difficulty may not be what an employer or customer wants to hear, but instead they would appreciate seeing the new improved you energetic, pleasant, decisive and able to deliver on your promises.

Who is in Charge?

While you are unemployed you can still be productive as you prepare yourself for a new life. Take charge of improving what you have to offer employers and customers alike. Work on things that would please a customer while working on things that satisfy an employer. An employer may have educational requirements a customer just wants a more pleasant shopping experience. What can you do that will satisfy customers and employers alike? Taking charge of listing those things that satisfy customers and employers may not change what you deliver today, but it makes you more aware of what you need to continue to work on every day. You may be asked by an employer what you have been doing while unemployed, recalling all your hardships is not the right answer unless you have used those hardships to make a positive difference in your life going forward.

While contracting with a large organization I met another contractor that did basically the same work I did for another project engineer. He was older and seemed very competent. Gerry confided in me that he was a recovering alcoholic and that he was just turning his life around. He asked about my background and what he might be able to do to improve his resume. I pointed out a number of affiliations I had that were helpful in the engineering community. While we worked on separate projects he would share with me the progress he had made in connecting with the engineering community and some of the credentials he was accumulating. I was impressed that he had taken control of his life in so many ways and made himself a better person and employee at the same time. At one point the company I was contracting with had an opening for a project engineer and I was told that the position was mine if I wanted it. I was told that if I did not take the job my friend Gerry would be offered the position. Well as luck would have it I had been working on another job opportunity and would pass on this one, but I was very pleased to know that Gerry would get the opportunity. When I left the organization I took many lessons with me including those shared with me by Gerry and his fight to take charge of his life and live to see a better life. His experience is not unique and has lessons for anyone impacted by someone that has had an alcoholic in their life either as a friend or as a family member.

Who is in Charge?

Take charge of the little things and the big things will come along for the ride. Improving your day to day situation may seem like a slow and monotonous process, but it is a path that many people have followed out of some really dark places in their life. If you are feeling overwhelmed by your situation working on daily objectives and goals is a good place to start.

Losing a job is not the problem it is finding a new job that makes life difficult. I have seen six recessions during my adult life and this one does seem to be the most severe relative to job loss. Digging out of this one may be a bit more difficult than the others, but there are many things in place to help the individual that were not as well developed in the last recession. The community colleges were not as well organized to help you learn new skills as they are today. The internet is much more mature than it was back in the early 1990's for business and personal use. Many more people are due to retire in the next few years, but some of the losses people have sustained may be deferring their retirement date. The question is how can the individual take advantage of the latest factors in this recession and get back to work?

Some of the best paying jobs today do not require a college education, but they do require some training that is probably available at your local community college. If you are considering going into small business the community colleges are offering informal classes for entrepreneurs. Even though unemployment is still near ten percent the Gross Domestic Product in this country is still well over fourteen trillion dollars. People are buying and selling things and you need to find a way to participate.

What about that path of least resistance? The worst case of following the path of least resistance will lead to doing the wrong thing. However there is another path of least resistance, it includes preparing a plan to minimize risk, evaluating the match between you and an employer or customer and targeting opportunity that is currently available. Resistance becomes support when it is works to maintain positive gains. If you are trying to overcome the resistance someone has to buying a product or service once you have made the sale their resistance now becomes support for your product or service and resistance to others. If you are trying to overcome an employers resistance to hire you once they hire you they have invested in you as an employee and they resist hiring another in your place.

Finding the path of least resistance may require finding the best time to make your pitch for the customer or the employer. High resistance is an indicator that the timing is not right for some unknown reason. This is a time when many employers and customers are resistant to either hiring new people or buying new products, because they are lack confidence in their ability to afford to pay for the expense short term. How do you promote what you have to sell? What is the return on investment? If you are selling a product that insures security against theft you are proposing that the return on investment is against the cost of loosing valuables. If you have experience waiting on upset customers at a service counter the return on investment you provide is that of not offending the paying customer. Most sales are made to returning customers not new customers. Treating dissatisfied customers with respect insures they return to the business and spend the amount refunded and more. Find the path of least resistance by considering and promoting how the employer or customer can benefit by considering what you have to offer.

Some of the most sought after products and people have value that was not promoted in so many words. Instead the promotion was in the form of an image that was portrayed in an advertisement. When it comes to an employer or a customer you are your best promotion. Your appearance is a first impression that may close the deal or build resistance from that first contact. How you interact with the employer or customer is another promotion that will either reduce resistance or build resistance to what you have to offer. For these reasons preparation is important. Are there changes you need to make that require you to take control over your actions? Learn presentation by either examining your own experience or by learning from others. How someone or something is presented to the prospective buyer is important enough to spend time and resources to get it right before making your next pitch for a job or a sale. Take control and responsibility for how you present yourself to employers and customers, by changing the message your appearance sends.

Appearances are not everything they just happen to give people their first opportunity to evaluate you before you say a word. If your appearance is acceptable you may get an opportunity to promote yourself or a product. I mentioned before that I have bought and sold to people around the world that I have never met. How does appearance impact that relationship? Well whatever the point of contact is a website, a trading platform, a storefront or a newspaper ad that point of contact represents you. The presentation becomes more sophisticated because it is more difficult to understand what satisfies the majority of people that will choose to do business with you. It never the less represents the first impression that people have of you.

You can lower resistance and improve the odds of acceptance and support by taking charge of making a good first impression and follow it up with an outstanding customer experience. That is the path of least resistance I refer to as compared to the path of poor choices that is usually implied by taking the path of least resistance. When you get signals of resistance let it be a warning that you need to review your plan. Likewise embrace support that comes once resistance is overcome. Review why resistance has changed to support? What have you done that would merit support? Usually there is a moment during a presentation for a customer or an interview with an employer that you get a signal that you have connected and they agree with what you propose. You then summarize your pitch and ask for their commitment to close the deal. If you were right and the customer or employer commits note the moment and what made the sale. It will probably be a factor as you try to close other sales.

All customers have different needs, but usually a product a service or your skills have limited application relative to the customer. Finding a niche will probably yield better pay and make you memorable to the customer or the employer. Before computers were used for the purpose of rotating design elements in space it could be done manually using a discipline called descriptive geometry. I learned this discipline and used it so frequently I assumed that any designer could do this if asked. To my surprise a particular client I had would pay me about three times my normal rate to provide just that part of the work and hand off the balance of work to other less skilled designers. Secondarily I found other clients that would hire me just to review the finished work of others in a methodical way that would correct errors and insure the quality of the less than complete work that others would generate. These are examples of niches that provided me months of work at relatively high pay. Finding a niche that you satisfy might accelerate your ability to move up the pay scale, because you save a customer time, or money quickly.

The essence of taking control or taking charge of your action is establishing habits that carry you toward success. Even when you are not focused on an accomplishment those habits tend to lay the groundwork for another opportunity. Some of the most routine tasks can lead to some of the biggest rewards. When I established good eating and activity habits I lost 60 pounds. When I established a low debt habit I reduced my debt without increasing my income. When I established a positive cash flow habit I increased my assets without increasing my income. When I established a habit of looking for opportunities to increase my income I found work both as an employee and as a self employed person. When I established a habit for learning I completed two four year trade school programs, the ability develop computer programs, and a bachelor degree at an accredited college. When I established the habit of instructing people around me I was paid as an instructor by small and large companies. When I established the habit of listening to people around me I grew closer to my family. When I developed a habit of writing I wrote three books.

Every day there are new opportunities to take charge and control of your life. You may need to determine a direction to take in the future or change the direction you are headed. It is up to you to take charge of your actions. Your actions will influence the success you can look back on or forward to today and years from now. Always start small even if you have big dreams to establish those habits that will lead you to success.

Who is in Charge?

Over the years I have observed many people that have succeeded and they all to a person were in charge of the events in their lives. They all had frustrating moments but were all able to work through their frustration to succeed despite their fear of failure. When they were overwhelmed by events they fell back on the habits that had brought them success in the past and worked through the difficult periods of their lives to succeed once again. Some had weathered significant losses that had measurably changed their lives, but they came through it with remarkable energy to succeed again. Everyone can find examples of other people that face challenges greater than their own to give them motivation to do the hard day to day work that establishing good habits require.

One of the many remarkable people I have had the fortune to meet was a fellow designer. I had already completed my apprenticeship while he was just beginning his training. I was in my twenties and he was nearly forty. As I worked with him I found out his previous work was as a cook. Although the group of designers we worked with tended to be rather competitive and unforgiving of shoddy work if you showed some measure of humility they were more than happy to give you direction. "Stretch" as we like to call him, a nick name that referred to his height, may not have had a background in the design world as so many new apprentices had but he did have humility. That one character trait served him well, because despite the difficulty he experienced throughout the apprenticeship once he achieved journeyman status he found an appropriate niche for his skill level and succeeded like all the other designers around him never losing his humble approach to his work and other people.

Being in charge or in control does not mean becoming obnoxious and pushy. So if you are more of a laid back person do not confuse control or being in charge with behavior that is not a normal part of who you are. You still need to take initiative and follow through on your plans, but it all can be done by the meek as well as the bold. Humility does not make an unemployed person more likely to accept unemployment, but it probably makes unemployment less traumatic when it happens. As a self employed person you may need to be a bit more gregarious than you would as an employee, but it is another opportunity to grow and learn more about yourself.

Make unemployment a challenge like any other and take action to overcome it like you would a weight problem or a smoking habit. You may need to ask for help overcoming unemployment just like any other problem that needs to be addressed in your life, but being in charge of the effort will give you the confidence that is needed to get a job or become self employed. Be humble in your approach to overcoming your joblessness, but tenacious in your resolve to become employed. Adding humility to your approach will prepare you to learn from your experience, seek understanding, training and education as may be required.

Different environments foster different temperaments, but the full range of emotion is usually present anywhere you find people. Channeling the energy of your emotions into a productive use of your time applies while you are unemployed as well as when you have work and things seem to be in your favor. When you are unemployed even if every day has a plan, without work you may still feel a bit out of control. Sometimes the best way to regain a sense of control is to take a break from it. I do not mean let your life spiral out of control, but instead take a break from trying to make things happen long enough to observe what is actually happening. It is a way of gaining new perspective that will influence your next action. Regardless of how desperate your situation may be the best plan to recover is one that depends on steady progress toward the objectives and goals you have established. Use your emotional moments to energize the work that needs to be done to prepare you for that next opportunity to succeed at a job or in a business.

Some people make the mistake of thinking that their control needs to extend to other people. As an unemployed person nothing could be more destructive to your effort to get employed than an effort to control others. It is a trait that tends to drive away employers and customers alike. Controlling behavior by anyone will not energize them, but instead drain them of the energy they have. If you are unemployed consider giving up on controlling others as a way to conserve energy for the important work you need to do every day to make a difference in your own life.

Who is in Charge?

Controlling behavior may be a bad habit but it can be overcome if you can find a way to reward yourself for avoiding it one day at a time. Become an observer of other people instead of a participant that tries to redirect their lives. If you are asked for an opinion you can share it, but emphasize it is only one persons' opinion. The only thing worse than being a controlling person, is being subjected to someone with that behavior. A controlling person will always gravitate to those that let them have control. Breaking the grip of a controlling person can be difficult, so it is best done incrementally. If you find yourself unemployed and dependent on a rather controlling person you need to move on. Preserve a say over what you need to do every day to provide yourself opportunity tomorrow.

I have known several people that were very controlling individuals and surprisingly they were at both ends of the prosperity spectrum. One with little or nothing to show for their life experience lived in a mental asylum for the last part of her life. She lived a life manipulating family and friends until all around her was chaos. Those family and friends after many second chances abandon her and left her to the streets. She spiraled out of control becoming a danger to herself and others around her that lead to her life in a mental institution. I have lost touch with those that knew her and I have no idea how they have put her life into perspective. The other person I know quite well and have witnessed the carnage around his life. There was a time when he did quite well and seemed on top of the world. Although he still continues to manipulate the lives around him he has sacrificed all those around him in an attempt to regain the glory he once possessed. The lesson here is take control of your life, but stop short of controlling others unless it is thrust upon you. If you are in a relationship with a controlling person, work to make a life that depends on your decisions.

Chapter 4

Where is the Motivation?

The motivation to move heaven and earth to get work that can support you and perhaps a family is within you. No one else can assemble the emotion that ultimately will give you the drive that keeps you up late or gets you up early. It will be you in the end that gives the employer or the customer a reason to pick you over all other choices. Fuel your motivation with something that is external and separate from you, because the fuel must always be within reach and common to all business big and small. That something is the customer.

After months of what seems like a futile search for work what gets your head off the pillow and back to seeking that next opportunity? How do you establish that fire within that fuels the extra effort that takes you from being a runner up to being in first place? You will need to connect with a customer to win a sale. First just tell yourself that each potential customer will have your full attention. Customers signal you through the entire conversation if they are prepared to buy what you are selling. The question is, are you listening while you are making the pitch? The customer or employer, that is an internal customer, needs to be what directs how, what, when and where you try to make a sale.

If you are not aware of what the customer or employer is looking for in a detailed way before you start to speak, you may be wasting their time and yours. Do some real homework before you make your next pitch for a job or a sale. If you need to talk to someone on the inside to understand the business better, visit the business as a potential customer and ask some questions. If it is a customer you seek be the customer.

Selling yourself or your ability is more art than science, knowing the product or service detail is the science part and knowing the customer is the art. Products and services can be technical and complicated, but knowing how to engage the customer takes wisdom beyond technical understanding. You can

Where is the Motivation?

attend classes that help you learn to sell, but whatever you learn will need to be tested. Before you sign up for some eight weeks of schooling try this simple method of learning from your experience. Since you have already met many employers and many customers start with making a short list of what part of any interview or conversation went best. These are the moments you personally connected with an employer or a customer. Getting an employer or customer interested is a little like trying to start a fire you need to discover how to make a spark that will grow to be a flame. That list of what went well describes the sparks you personally generate. The next interview needs to include as many of those moments as possible. It might be as simple as being cordial polite and quick to explain how you can help. Always know how you can help make a positive difference. Leave the potential employer or customer with information that allows them to make some consideration of what you offer. You need to offer something that is easily described, competitively priced, and readily available with a promotion any customer can take advantage of today.

Why not use more personal motivations such as a need to support and feed yourself and your family? Translating those motivations into getting or keeping a job do not usually connect you to the person paying you for your work. People that express the need to work for their family and the material gains they may achieve usually have a difficult time explaining why the customer should care about satisfying those things. However, zeroing in on what connects with the customer will give you positive feedback and sustain you in the work you need to do every day to both find work or keep a job after you get it. Furthermore you always have a customer based reason for what you do to reinforce the work you do all day long. Personal reasons for work will vary in strength and in substance from one person to another, but the customer will generate a level of intensity in line with today's market. As a business person you will naturally be closer to understanding the customer, but as an employee you likewise need to be engaged in satisfying the customer at some level.

I like so many business people I have known seem to get energized by engaging a customer one on one and negotiating what

Where is the Motivation?

will close the sale. In those moments you realize that the customer generally has some basic requirements, but giving them a personal reason for selecting you as the supplier is what will make the sale. Some customers are concerned that the specifications will be so detailed that any necessary last minute changes will force them to accept unusually high costs or settle for a less than satisfactory product. There are points in any process that commitment needs to be firm, but being as flexible and as engaging as possible will not change the price. Giving the customer consideration and understanding their constraints is usually the key to making a sale that will lead to additional sales.

Over the past dozen years I have had occasion to need the services of an auto collision repair shop. I shopped around and compared prices and facilities. The latest collision shop that I have done business with has been so accommodating in both price and quality of service that I have repeatedly used and recommended their service for the last three years. I am never pleased that I have occasion to need the work done, but I am always comforted by the consistent service I get even from people that are on the job for the first day. I do not know any of these people personally and I am sure they all have complicated lives, but they are customer focused. The facility is clean efficient and if I need to spend more than a few minutes there I could make myself comfortable. I have noticed the same customer accommodations at my favorite car dealerships, restaurants, retail stores and dentist office. It is not the specific type of business that happens to get the combination right, but any business that is customer driven.

The same is true of employees I have worked with or people I have met over the years. Those people that have a customer focus are usually rewarded by being in demand. Being more accommodating and more engaged in getting customers what they need and want makes them a customer favorite. The customer wants a good experience and is usually willing to reward the business that gives them that good experience. Some of the best people I have worked with understood better than I that they derived motivation from developing a connection to their respective customers. The best example of this was two young men

Where is the Motivation?

that actually turned their ability to meet customer requirements into a friendly competition between themselves. The measure of success was the hours from start to finish they would consume in meeting the customers requirements. I never saw two more energetic people competing on the job without any prompting from the management. Their talent to get the job done and energize others around them was rewarded over time. Both eventually were promoted to the plant manager position one following the other. They truly enjoyed the work they did and meeting customer requirements was always first in their mind.

If the customer doesn't motivate you as an employee it makes being in small business difficult until you realize that the only reason you are kept in business is because you are satisfying the customer. Enjoying the experience makes doing what it takes to get and keep customers much easier. If you hope to develop good habits consider being in the habit of serving the customer.

For centuries business people have always known they must have a product that serves the customer, at a price the customer will pay, available in a place the customer shops and promoted in a way that attracts the customer. Without reaching into the past, but instead pointing out how that applies today more than ever might be more useful. Consider products that sell today from the basics to the luxuries. Their place in the market although vital to the economy may promote sales of other products. Gasoline sales today seem to be a product sold only to attract people into stores that sell a wide variety of food and snacks. Movie houses may attract you to see the latest movie, but the real profit they make is on all the snacks you buy at the refreshment stand. Shoe stores still sell shoes and at a profit, but many sell handbags and sportswear at considerable profit as well. Grocery stores have taken to selling some of the oddest offerings televisions, lawn furniture snow shovels and those are not the super stores that have clothing and sports goods. That might explain some of the really high "grocery" bills.

Serving the customer never seems to be an old idea, because it is always successful in attracting new business. Web sites that have do-it-yourself ways of providing customers with answers

Where is the Motivation?

before they buy save hours of personal contact that may or may not make a sale. My most recent use of such a website was in outfitting a closet with shelves, drawers and hanger space. I along with my wife configured the closet space over and over until we agreed on a configuration that served our purpose. The precut elements are precise and are delivered at a fraction of the price we would have paid to have a cabinet maker build the same configuration. Yes it will require some work on my part, but we can do it at our own pace and at a time that is convenient to us. We personally use nothing less than a dozen web sites regularly for shopping and entertainment. Likewise we visit many stores and restaurants so the place we do business varies but the thing we seek is a good experience and products that are priced right. If we get a promotional price or consideration that brings us back again it only enhances the experience.

Personal motivation needs to fit with your willingness to serve the customer everyday either as an employee or as a business person. What are you doing everyday that a customer will reward you for? Waiters and waitresses are a group of people that get regular feedback from customers and depend on them to be rewarded for good service. Other jobs likewise depend on bonuses that are many times based on the strength of the business the customer provides. The further you get from the front door of a business the more you tend to serve internal customers. This can be very destructive to the larger business, because internal customers do not always have the external customer in mind when they generate a request. Businesses that do not allow there to be a differential between the external and internal customers usually profit greatly. As an unemployed person it can be difficult focusing on a nonexistent customer, so focus on the potential customer. Any business you hope to work for has known customers. When you apply for a job at that company know who they are and be able to talk about them to the interviewer. If you choose instead to become a small business you must identify the potential customers you hope to serve and focus on their needs.

A real advantage of focusing on the customer for your motivation is the ability to be more objective about what you need to do to satisfy them as compared to some of your personal motivations that get confused with the customer. You may want a lot of things to make life satisfying, but what do you really need to make gains on a personal basis? When you are evaluating a customer request you already know what your product or service was meant to satisfy, and deciding if the customer is reasonable or not is fairly easy. When the request for something comes from your family for some reason what you provide is more difficult to decide. If it is something you personally want separating wants and needs may come down to what is affordable. Turn that around and make your wants into customer requests to decide how reasonable they are as compared to the lengths you will go to satisfy the request. For example you want a new automobile. If the request came from a business associate that made sales calls for the company you run, what would your response be? It seems to me that you would have more questions for the business associate than you would have had for yourself.

For a long time I denied the importance of the customer. While it was self employment that got me to address the customer needs, it was a search for employment that got me there. As the employment picture has deteriorated over the past years and months it has reminded me of those early years when I was unemployed and seeking a more stable situation. Every time a recession occurs it provides new opportunity for people to discover that customer motivation that can change their life. I do not know how this disconnect between people and customers contributes to a recession, but as people connect with customers and find work prosperity seems to emerge from every recession I have experienced over the past 50 years.

Focusing on satisfying customers will never be a lost effort, because whenever you do find employment you will need to apply what you have learned. As an unemployed person there is always a concern that every effort not be wasted. When you work to satisfy a potential customer the effort is not lost if the customer moves on, because the effort will serve your next customer. So spend time identifying the customers you want to serve and what they are likely to list as their needs and wants. When you connect with a customer,

Where is the Motivation?

notice the things that made that sale a success. Was the product the key to the sale? Did the price you were able to offer make the difference? Was it availability at a familiar shopping place that sold the customer? Was there a unique promotion that the customer wanted to take advantage of at that time? These may be the keys to the next of many more sales to come if you can emphasize the elements of a successful sale.

Just as I search for good news and examples of ways you can apply a new approach to motivation the reality of the unemployment numbers are being reported today. Unemployment rises to 10.2 percent from 9.8 percent and the total unemployment is estimated at 17.5 to 18 percent on Friday November 6, 2009. These numbers are being compared to the recession of 1983 and my recollection of 1983 was not as grim as I view what is going on today. The Chrysler Corporation was struggling much like it is today and work in the Detroit, Michigan area was scarce, but the other automakers were getting by despite losses. The question is, when will a monthly loss of jobs turn positive? For you it could be today even if the job losses continue to increase for a while. How can I say that with any real authority? It is not enough to have lived through several of these downturns to see the prosperity on the other side. It is my current observation of the businesses that succeed in these times that gives me a positive perspective in a recovery that will eventually happen. All the statistics may point to a jobless recovery, but even a jobless recovery does not rule out your potential as a small business of one or more employees. As a matter of fact a large part of recession recovery is new small business.

This recession will not be different in that respect. For those people interested in getting back to work they may need to opt for self employment over being employed by someone else, even though many jobs have been lost in small business. There are some real advantages such as being more interested in the work you do every day, or having a diverse number of tasks throughout the day. I would suggest these are not small differences, because they take your life in a different direction. You will be constantly learning more about the business you are in as well as more about yourself every day. It will require you to find energy you may never have had in the past or it may renew the energy you have had but lost. The disadvantages will seem minor as compared to being unemployed for an extended period of time. Oh did I mention that many of the jobs being lost are being lost in small business? Yes I did, just trying to see if you were paying attention.

Remember as a business of one person you are less than a small business; you are a micro business. You won't even be a statistic until you hire someone other than yourself. So you may want to remain under the radar of the bean counters and statisticians for a while just to avoid junk mail that will hunt you down even if you change your address. As a micro business that can sustain itself and grow you will enjoy many of the benefits of being in business without some of the negatives that small businesses are currently experiencing. You won't be shedding any jobs if you are the only employee. You won't be concerned that some business smaller than you is taking your customers, unless you are competing with someone in school that is doing the same thing to raise money for a charity. All joking aside there is a place for one person part time and full time self employment. Usually these businesses develop a network of people that use the service as a convenience and tell others that in turn will likewise make occasional use of the service. A good example of this is a seamstress that occasionally alters clothing for my wife. She always seems available, but usually is just finishing another order as she takes on new work. She is well into her 90's and lives independently in a small condominium. These people have found a niche that provides them sufficient income without the burden of directing other people. They prosper as other people discover the convenience of using their service that usually requires some knowledge or skill. They are usually people that do not have expensive tastes and habits and pass some of that savings on to their customers.

So no matter how small a business you are you must give that customer a reason to come back again and again, because 80 percent of your business will be from twenty percent of your best customers. This is perhaps another application of the Pareto principle named after the Italian economist Vilferdo Pareto. All business will depend on repeat business and the best way to ensure

Where is the Motivation?

repeat business is to give your customer some reason to choose you over larger and more established business. The reasons can vary but they will probably be the same reasons that you choose one larger business over another of its same size. Most customers will be sensitive to customer service from the largest to the smallest business. Make the customer your focus and listen to their requirements before you promise to deliver something that does not meet their needs.

The statistics are not good regarding jobs today, but by the time you read this the statistics will probably have improved. Of course the banks will probably continue to fail a 120 so far in 2009 as of today November 7,2009. Meanwhile we need to focus on motivation to move forward and secure work in a tough business climate. Does motivation allow you to ignore all of the negative indicators that continue to emerge? No, instead motivation should help you engage the information and avoid some of the disasters while taking advantage of the limited opportunities that emerge along the way. What opportunities? Well when unemployment rises to the highest levels in 26 years and many of the state and local governments have geared up to help train and retrain people that have lost jobs through the community college programs there are a lot of people attending classes that need a variety of support. Does this emphasis translate into consumer purchases?

What are working customers buying? "Consumers are being attracted by what prices are. Unless they feel that they're getting a good value for their money they won't shop," Jharonne Martis, director of consumer research for Thomas Reuters as reported by the International Business Times November 5 of 2009 by Nicole Maestri. A more general statement of what people are buying can be found at the government site that collects statistics on consumer purchases at http://www.census.gov/retail . As you look at the details of the report for September 2009 the shift in seasonal sales is apparent, but a large increase in items that focus on the impact of unemployment seems to be absent except for sluggish sales in general. Unemployment does limit the revenue growth of everything from small business to large business and government coffers as well.

Where is the Motivation?

This means when it comes to looking for opportunities highlighted by the retail sales report, it should begin with the sales to people that are still employed and looking for bargain prices to make their money go further. They are still 80 percent or more of the people making purchases. It is sometimes hard to remember that the customer is the person still buying when you are part of a growing group of unemployed people. As a small business person looking to sell to the greatest number of customers your focus needs to be on the consumers still holding jobs unless the only population you serve is the unemployed. When you aim to serve the working customer there are going to be a number of unemployed within the customers you serve. In turn you serve the greatest number as compared to aim for a smaller niche. Let your product or service determine the customer niche, for example if you sell lawnmowers you will naturally serve homeowners for the most part. The report does reveal a slight increase in the sales of general merchandise. Looking to the media for sales that have created opportunity would reveal certain electronic games and devices that have had outstanding sales. The media has also called attention to the thrift store sales that seem to be booming in these difficult times. The question is what is a fit for you? Can you sell yourself first and then anything else you might have a liking for or do you need a product that is a bigger part of you? If you have a special skill or liking for certain products or services your passion is more easily expressed and passed on to the customer.

It is times like these that your energy is a big part of what you sell, because people are looking for something to be enthusiastic about even if it is a rug cleaning service. The possibilities are too numerous to mention, because they are only limited to your imagination. Consider those moments that you have connected with people in a conversation and transferred some of your energy to them. Customers looking to share that energy will stand in line to buy what you sell if only you can identify it and make it a part of what you sell. If you can focus on the customer when the customer connects with what you sell it becomes an unstoppable combination for motivation that can only lead to your success. Take your motivation to the street. Do not contain yourself in a way that bottles up that enthusiasm that customers are eager to

Where is the Motivation?

see feel and touch. Be the best example of how your product or service energizes someone that is totally sold and can explain the benefits to anyone that wants to know more about what you have to sell.

Customers of a depressed market will gravitate toward someone that rejuvenates their energy. Be the person that customers want to be with, and they will buy your product or service. Your motivation may start with the customer, but it needs to include what you sell. Your enthusiasm needs to connect the customer and your product or service in a way that the customer agrees with instantly. Knowing yourself and how your product or service can be of value to potential customers is the homework you need to do before you make your first pitch. Practicing your delivery will be part of that homework. You must be prepared to speak in short simple phrases that make valuable points that get the interest of potential customers. Be prepared for the customer to interrupt your pitch, but be willing to talk the customer to the finish line if required by asking questions along the way. If the customer interrupts you to ask a question use the opportunity to customize your pitch for that customer. Making what you sell more relevant to the customer will help you make the sale, so do not discourage questions.

A strange thing happened to me on my way to an interview with a prospective employer. I decided to offer my services on a contract basis instead of as a hired employee. I had never done this before, but knew of others that had been doing it successfully for years. To my surprise the employer was open to the proposal and hired me that day. It was a time when few jobs were available back in the 1980's and engineering companies were minimizing the hired staff while finding ways to hire sufficient people temporarily to complete medium size projects. The job was not advertized but was the result of a number of "cold calls" I made earlier in the week. I had researched the names of companies that had recently won engineering contracts from a source inside a larger company. Knowing that the contracts were not open ended, but only of medium duration I suspected that these companies would only need help for a short time. As it was that contract lasted for six months

Where is the Motivation?

and after a two month pause was renewed for another year. The customer was initially sold on the terms of my employment and secondarily satisfied by my on the job performance sufficient to renew my contract. Connecting with the customer on terms, price and performance provided me with a living for a year and a half. For me that was a rather enlightening experience. Today employers are likewise stressed to get work done without incurring obligations that go beyond their short term contracts.

Look for opportunities to service other business with products and services they need at great prices for special consideration. The one thing many businesses are having a hard time doing these days is paying for the services they need to buy. The last thing you need as a small business just getting started is someone that fails to pay their bill. You can research companies to find those that deserve more credit than others but at some point you will invest time and perhaps money in delivering a product that may not get paid for from 30 to 90 days. By offering an exceptional price you may be able to shorten the terms of your payment. Negotiate shortened terms of payment to improve your cash flow and to guard against other businesses failing unexpectedly.

Dealing with the general public directly can be a challenge, but it is another way to get cash payment on delivery of your product or service. Keeping your price competitive will help motivate customers to make cash payment and improve your cash flow position. Starting a micro business or one person operation when you are unemployed must limit the losses and maximize the gains every day. As a one person operation in a poor business environment gives you advantages that other businesses cannot match unless they structure the business around vendor services. Using vendors to expand your capacity may sacrifice some profit when times are good, but in the current business environment it is insurance against the loss of contracts that are short term. Having plug in vendor services may offer the micro business an easy migration to a larger small business structure. Vendor services need to be scrutinized for quality and on time delivery ahead of time to avoid production disasters that may ruin your reputation for quality and an ability to deliver on time. The customer does not want to hear you complain about vendors when you cannot deliver. As you pick your vendors do not forget your customer. The best price and quality comes from someone with a track record for producing even if you pay a slight premium.

Today with the array of services that individuals and businesses alike have to choose from it is very possible to put together a fairly robust business from a set of coordinated services. Well coordinated businesses complete some part of a larger job for the customer. Housing construction although still struggling to regain customers has over the years segmented into many specialized component parts. A single builder calls on one company to survey the property, another to excavate the foundation or basement, someone else sets the forms and pours the foundation or basement. The series of contractors is specialized and numerous through completion of the project. Other industries have used this construction project model to provide numerous other products and services. Some examples include building computers from a vast number of supplier parts and software, healthcare that depends on many specialist and specialized services, manufacturing although outsourced to many foreign nations is a network of thousands of companies that may be needed to complete one larger product such as an automobile. Every one of these products or services and many more that I have not mentioned provide opportunity for you if you are unemployed and seek to either get a job or start a business.

Knowing what customers are seeking in any given geographic area and what their expectations are should be the information you seek before you either approach a business for a job or a customer for their business. Doing your homework is the difference between endless searching and standing in long lines for consideration as compared to making a quick sale or being pursued for what you provide for customers. Yes it is more difficult in the bad business environment we find ourselves in today, but only because it requires greater focus, fewer mistakes and energy that can get you over the finish line every day. Let the customer give you the energy, they are everywhere, they have energy when you don't and they possess the requirements and cash to pay your way in the world. If you lack direction try to decide which customers you want

Where is the Motivation?

to do business with every day. Actually prepare a profile that describes the customer. If the customer you seek is numerous they need not have deep pockets, but if the customers you seek are rare they must be willing to provide you with large commissions on what you sell. Doing research on customers might be as simple as learning the fundamentals of a business or even simple observation of other people doing their job.

Simple observation may not get you to the details without some questioning, but it can let you know more about the environment you would be expected to perform in. Fundamentals will be sufficient if the work is straight forward such as buying and selling. The complications of buying and selling vary, from simple to complicated, depending on the product or service you choose to buy or sell. You must decide where you invest your energy. Do you invest in making a complicated selling process simple for the customer to get through more simply, or do you invest in the customer contact experience and demonstrating a simple basic product that meets your customer needs.

Rather than running from one employer to another looking for that one business that has room and money to pay you, consider the customer you would serve and feed yourself for many years to come. Once you have a customer in mind getting a job or starting a business seems more ordinary than extraordinary. So many people that are unemployed are focused on the next job and not the next customer. It is the customer that needs to be the focus of an unemployed person. The customer can generate energy to do things like learn a skill or become more knowledgeable about a service or product. Without the customer you spend your energy aimlessly acquiring what you think you need to land a job. With the customer in mind you draw energy from them as you consider what they want to buy.

Is the customer looking for a familiar product or service at a reasonable price? Is the customer looking for someone that can help them make a decision? When you offer a product or a service the customer usually has other more familiar providers in mind to draw comparisons from to evaluate what you have to offer. Help the customer make comparisons that improve your sale. Providing

Where is the Motivation?

a better price and a more convenient experience may be the difference between yes and no when you move to close a sale. As odd as it might seem I have been approached by door to door salespeople that are selling thousands of dollars worth of furniture from the back of a 18 wheel tractor trailer. The customer that does buy is looking for that single piece or set of pieces that closely match what they have searched endless stores looking for never being satisfied with the price. Here the sales person that has in many cases name brand furniture brings the store to the shopper and slightly enhances the price. Although I have never bought anything from these vendors, I always give them consideration. Others in my neighborhood have bought and have been satisfied with their purchases. Only you can construct a new offer that the customer may or may not find appropriate, but the process starts with giving the customer consideration.

Exciting the customer is not an easy thing when so many products exist. Pitchmen in television commercials apply a formula of sorts that makes the product they offer a bit unique. The most successful products usually include quality, simple application and a price or payment plan that the average consumer can afford. The formula only works after the sales person connects with the customer. With all the distractions in our environment getting the attention of the customer can be quite a challenge. What are sales people in your neighborhood doing to connect with the customer that works? What works in my neighborhood may not work where you live. The best current example of this is housing. Home construction is generally depressed throughout the country, but specific markets have done well this year as compared to last year. Last year, 2008, one home was built in my subdivision this year nearly three dozen have been built with more to come. That is a dramatic increase. Many people are predicting another slump at the end of this year along with continuing unemployment and the worst plummeting commercial property returns since 1978, Investment Property Database, www.ipd.com . What works in one neighborhood may also change from day to day or week to week. Follow the customer and their spending habits to get their consideration no matter how things change the customer will always be the target of consideration.

Where is the Motivation?

As a one person business that needs to quickly determine what your customer thinks everyday question your customers often and directly to learn what you need to know. Polls and surveys are effective for larger businesses that may not have the customer standing in front of them, but that does not describe an unemployed person seeking work. Cold calling and door to door selling are usually a brutal experience, but a refinement of that is a vendor at a portable stand that is organized for vendors. An open air market, a garage sale, an online auction or maybe a three line add in a local newspaper all are good alternatives to the cold call or the door to door sale routine. There are also two or three day store fronts organized around a holiday to sell holiday related items. These are all situations that demand customer interaction and each can shape your response to questions if you are truly interested in satisfying the customer.

When a customer questions the price answer with alternate plans that allow you to provide some part of what you sell for a price they see as within their budget. If a customer questions quality, explain their options for repair replacement or refund should the product fail. You only succeed if the customer is satisfied and returns for more or refers your product or service to others. It will surprise you how many of the questions from customers remain the same. Once you have fielded a fair number of questions your answers will be quick and to the point giving the customer time to ask more questions or to make their purchase.

Successful businesses small and large connect with the customer every time they sell especially in a depressed market. They always need to review where those sales came from to determine if it was a repeatable experience. What is the best reason for the success? It is always the customer. Maintaining the customer connection during good times and bad maximizes gains and minimizes losses. If a business detects discounted sales promote business they need to balance that against what money is available for promotion, because promotion is a cost that reduces profit. It is not enough to drop prices, because giving profits away is not a way to make profits. As an unemployed person you may take advantage of discount prices to improve your budget, but you cannot spend endlessly on discounted products you may or may not use. As an unemployed person you can discount the product or service you offer a customer, but like any business the discount you offer has real limits. The best deals you can make are the ones you can agree to repeatedly. If the first customer is satisfied can you offer it to the next customer? Can you make the same offer over time as prices rise?

Establishing moment to moment motivation is important to getting started, but establishing weekly and monthly motivation is important to an enduring success. Let's look at the moment to moment ways to either get or stay motivated. When you do not have direct contact with the customer taking time to consider how what you are doing serves the next customer is important to staying engaged and motivated. When you have direct contact with the customer listen more closely to the customer and paraphrase their statements to clarify what they are telling you to improve the customer connection. Make it a way of doing business to get in business and to stay in business. If your customer is somewhat removed from you personally look very carefully at the signals the customer sends you over time on a minute to minute, hour to hour, or even a day to day basis. As you look back over the past week or month search for action that has resulted in a better customer connection even if it did not lead to an immediate sale of product or service. Identifying the signals that make you a profit instead costing you a loss will be technical indications that you are anticipating the customer. If your customers buy what you sell over the internet or over the telephone you may never have a face to face meeting, but the sales results you generate need to be your guide to success.

If you have limited success, use the results to model greater success. The more difficult it is to profit in your chosen endeavor the more likely there are technical indications that you are not proceeding in the right direction. These technical indicators are probably obvious to someone that is seasoned and successful in that field, and less obvious or even unknown to the novice. Let your level of sustained success determine where you place on the scale that measures expertise. It should be a humbling experience

Where is the Motivation?

barring some level of unusual luck. For example five years of experience does not always translate into expert level of understanding and five days of good fortune does not mean you are a natural. Average your success over weeks, months and years to evaluate your level of expertise. If there are periods of sustained success look for a pattern of behavior that you can repeat to follow a clearly defined process for success. Understand that risk is always present and failure is occasional, but identifying a method for minimizing failures and minimizing losses to achieve steady growth and profit is part of what needs to be done. The other part is to manage increased risk during successful periods and minimize risk during periods of loss to leverage your success. Just like a long lever can help a small person move a big rock using leverage to achieve business goals and employment opportunities is a must.

When a customer motivates you it needs to be followed up with swift and vigorous action to close the sale and ring up a profit. If some of this seems a bit fuzzy and difficult to translate into your life and your experience let me give you some real examples of leveraging your success with a process that takes advantage of the successful periods in your life. First identify a single favorite time in your life when things seemed to work. Remember all things are relative, in other words what was a good experience for one person may be described as a miserable experience for another, so do not compare your favorite experience with that of other people just yet. Once you have identified that time in your life try to zero in on a single event that went well that you would like to capture and savor, because it made you feel good. This will be different for every person although there may be similar situations the names and the faces are unique to you. Now identify the customer and the service provider. If you are the customer in the situation make a detailed list of what the service provider did to make your experience memorable. If you were the service provider, what feedback from the customer made the experience a good one for you as well as the customer? In summary you have identified a potential business opportunity, the customer and why the customer was satisfied.

The next consideration you need to make is how does that business opportunity fit in today? If the opportunity has become

Where is the Motivation?

obsolete due to technology, or some combination of changes in how business is done today review similar services or products to find a better fit for the world you face today. Usually the experience you have had has an equivalent in business today. It may require you to consider a new business you are not familiar with that will take some learning before setting up. With one single good experience you are able to sift through all the noise that tries to push you one way or another toward full employment and find a path that is unique to you. It needs to be a path that you choose not one chosen for you only because there will always be obstacles that block your progress from time to time and working to overcome them will take more than a casual effort. You will need to depend on yourself like never before and find the ability to make things happen. It will not be wishing or wanting that will get you what you desire it will be taking action and overcoming failure until your success cannot be denied. Choosing the direction you will take makes the difficult less difficult and allows you to find reasoning that only applies to you when a reason to continue is hard to come by.

The customer must be known by you and if in your example the customer was you it will be easier to search for what satisfied the customer. If in your example you provided service or a product for someone you will need to recall why it pleased the customer and make an effort to nurture those types of circumstances in the business you plan to do from this day on. If the customer is happy you too will be happy. Satisfying the customer and looking for those things that will satisfy the customer should be your focus if you are looking for satisfying experiences that motivate you in the future. Customers are a necessary part of any business equation and when you neglect the customer that variable can drive earnings negative.

A single experience in your life can be the kernel of an idea that provides you with a living for a long time, so pay attention to what the customer is willing to pay for and translate that into today's market possibilities. When you seem to lack all motivation the most likely place to find what you need is usually closer than you might think. Look at your life experience regardless of how

Where is the Motivation?

insignificant you might think it is and be confident there is probably something to be learned. If you doubt this look more closely at some of what is offered for sale every day. The range of items and services seems endless and from items you would never consider to items that are indispensable. If the variety boggles your mind and you don't know where to start, limit your selection to something that is not impacted by the season, or the weather. It is surprising how many things will be eliminated, but you must find one item or service that you can focus on for an unlimited period of time. The first success needs to be examined closely.

Was it just luck or did you satisfy the early analysis and plan for success that you spent time developing? Luck isn't a bad thing, but you may want to position yourself to gain by both good decisions and luck when it does occur. Planning doesn't need to be complicated it just needs to be done. If you can describe your plan for making your next dollar on a moments notice in 30 seconds or less you have a plan. The real question is how successful is that plan? Keep track of your success to the extent that it can be described as a percent of your effort. For example if you executed your plan 10 times and were successful 4 out of 10 times you could describe your rate of success as 40% successful. Measure your success as positive or negative. For example if the 40% success rate pays the cost of your materials plus expenses and leaves money available for the next opportunity you are cash flow positive. This can be complicated by large expenses to start a business that is why your expenditures need to be minimized in early efforts to start a business. Large expenses are paid for over time and need to be minimized for small new businesses.

If you have identified a product or service and are planning in a way that will measure your success you can always improve your plan over time. As an unemployed individual you can be relatively successful and never noticed by the business community unless you choose to call attention to yourself. There are many successful people that live a quiet and private life. Learning a new way to earn a living can be an exciting and challenging time, but the motivation needs to come from something that never goes away all together no matter how grim the employment statistics are.

Where is the Motivation?

That something is the customer, either a retail shopper or a business that buys what they need at a discount as part of some product or service they deliver at a price customers are willing to pay. Never forget a customer must pay for what you are selling on a regular basis over time for you to succeed. Customers can be found worldwide, so no matter how small you start consider the world as your marketplace. The customer shops worldwide so the competition, even for a one person business, will likewise be worldwide with few exceptions. Do not believe that a foreign company will not be able to serve your domestic customers, because they do it today in more ways than you have time to count. This should not discourage you but instead give you great satisfaction that when you succeed you succeed on much greater level than people twenty and thirty years ago. You succeed because you can compete with anyone in the world. Plan to do something to make a difference and refine the plan until it works for the customer and you.

Over the years I have had several unique experiences that have allowed me to enjoy a comfortable life for many consecutive years. When life interrupts one way of living I usually draw on a new experience to savor a few more years of the good life from some other unique experience. When I was young, grade school, math and science came easy. I was aware of this and tended to pay stricter attention to my math and science classes never knowing where or when I would use it. The furthest thing from my mind was earning a living or serving a customer. Out of necessity I developed a mechanical ability to repair the thing I could not afford to have someone else fix, such as my bike or my car. It was then that I became my own best customer, repairing things on a regular basis. Although I did some of the same repairs for money when asked by someone else to do what they needed done it did not occur to me that repair work could be my life long vocation. I did take more formal training to build tools, dies and machinery that did require that mechanical ability along with some understanding of math and science. While working in the tool and die industry , it always seemed like there was too much wait time between the time that required real thought and consideration and the next time that same thought and consideration was needed. I moved on to the design of tools, dies and machinery I built. It was much more satisfying, but still required many hours of mechanically assembling the finished product that required careful consideration.

When computers made it to the office desktop I quickly moved to make them a part of what I did for a living. The thought needed and the possibilities were endless. This account of what I have done over the years is not a prescription for others to follow, but instead one example of how constant change has not restricted my ability to find customers, but exactly the opposite. I have expanded the base of customers I have served over the years to enable me to constantly find work and new ways to earn a living that did not exist some years ago. Likewise if you are unemployed you need to seek today's customers and provide them with products and services that they seek in today's world.

Today's customers should be your motivation, because they will in turn provide you with everything material you desire. If you link a passion to do some particular type of work to satisfying the customer you will be satisfied to a much greater extent. Only you can determine what you are willing to do to satisfy a customer, so the results you achieve as compared to someone else will always be different. The comparisons of results are necessary to achieve sustained results, but don't let a bad day or two shape your future. The customer will reward you tomorrow if you come up with the right product or service. If you feel you have had a series of bad years not days it may mean that you have not been doing what needs to be done to get in touch with customers day to day. The way to get back in the game is to do just that, shed any notion of having all the answers and approach what needs to be done with a fresh perspective. Let what the customer says direct what you need to do instead of trying to second guess them ahead of clear signals from the customer.

Without repeating the statistics that paint a grim picture consider instead the businesses that continue to serve customers every day. Most depend on not one or two customers as would a one person business, but instead they depend on many customers that visit their place of business on a regular basis. If they can survive in today's economy so can you with a substantially smaller

Where is the Motivation?

set of bills to pay. If you need to negotiate your debts to a more manageable level do it in a timely way. Debt collectors will consume your time and resources and need to be avoided if at all possible. The customer may be cautious and spend sparingly, but you need to let them know that you can work with customers that want the most for their money. Do not make the mistake of extending credit you can't afford to loose. Some percentage of credit may become bad debt, so don't be to willing to extend credit to people that do not have a history of good credit. If you happen to be one of those with bad credit do everything possible to improve and protect it going forward. Although we could spend some time considering how good credit goes bad it is not a topic any customer wants to spend time on. The customer wants a clear and concise offer from you. After that, they will compare your offer to others and choose the one that satisfies them at that time. The way to stay in the game or to be a part of any market is to make your offer competitive not impossible to profit from anytime you make an offer. Be aware of the market prices and what you can expect. Find ways that you can reduce costs and give the customer an option to improve their pricing.

What motivates the customers you deal with everyday? If they are looking for a good price and yours is competitive ask if they want to save that money today? If they hesitate, let them know that whenever they are ready to buy you will give them a competitive price. It takes the pressure off the sale and establishes a connection worth their time. If you don't sell what they need point them in a direction that is helpful, you will be remembered the next time they need what you sell. Establishing a connection and building a relationship with the customer takes time, but it is part of every customer contact. Returning customers include people that did not buy anything the first, second and third time that they came to shop. If you treat all customers well they will remember you. Make the best of every customer contact and take note of why they decided to buy from you.

The day you discover the customers ability to motivate what you do to make a sale or complete a project is a day that can seem endless, because the customer will always be there tomorrow to do it again. The customer supports any business small or large. As you begin to listen to the customer for their description of a product or service they seek, it helps if you paraphrase the requirements back to the customer. Without a clear understanding of what the customer wants you will waste time, effort, and resources. Asking questions to eliminate items is not as efficient as listening closely to the initial order and double checking what they state they want. Observing customers is another energizing experience, if you are looking for ways to satisfy the customer and ways to be gratified in return. If a customer seems in a hurry expediting their sales experience is a way to sell more. If the customer seems puzzled and needs more information to make a decision be available. Interaction with a customer should be cordial and directed by the product or service the customer seeks. Many times the customer needs to sort through options and sales support can keep the business going. When you are with a customer reflect their energy to improve their shopping experience.

If you have customer traffic the job of selling and servicing the customer is made easier. If you need to find a customer and attract them to your business do the easiest things first. Some businesses go to great expense advertising without much return on their money. Experiment with different ways to attract customers before spending greatly on one mode of advertisement. Think about the marketing that gets your attention and ask others about their most memorable advertisements. Marketing is about more than advertising, it includes choosing the right product or service, placing it where customers are most likely to shop for it, pricing it right and finally doing the promotion that includes some advertising. The customer can make your day and you need to give them an opportunity to do that today.

Engaging the customer can be like pouring gasoline into an empty fuel tank. They may only be able to provide you with enough fuel to get you 5 miles down the road, but the next customer may fill you up and energize you for days. If you are without a job or something to do, find a customer and they will put you to work serving them while they fuel your motivation. Some of what you provide for any customer can have a price tag. As a small business person motivated by many things, let the customer identify what they are willing to pay for and include it with what you sell. If the customer demands a reason to paint their house when the only thing you sell is paint, ask the questions that will allow them to get the reasons they need to close the deal. That customer service may separate you from all other sales people that day ensuring you get the sale. If the customer has difficulty deciding between the many options that are offered find a way to walk them through the process in a way that helps them decide with your help. As a customer you would expect the support, so as the business person be ready to provide whatever closes the deal. Some customers may use the sales help to bolster their thinking and then move on to buy elsewhere. You can only sell what you have, so your assistance must support your product or service. Regardless of where your product or service is on the spectrum of things to buy you must know why it can satisfy the customer. Help the customer focus on what you sell and the reasons they need what you have to offer.

Getting motivated is a very personal experience that can very greatly from one person to the next. Although I would suggest the customer is the common fuel for all motivation in business, why is the experience so different from one person to the next? We need to remember that we each bring a different life experience to the business of serving the customer. If the combination of your experiences and any customer contact is less than positive examine the encounter. Was the customer unreasonable? Was the customer rude? Do you recall the encounter and what the customer was in search of related to a product or service? Many customer encounters get side tracked if the customer is in a hurry or upset by their current shopping experience. It is easy to focus on the side issues and get defensive if we think the customer is being critical of us personally or the business. Moving a customer conversation toward what resolves their discontent takes time and practice. If you hope to be motivated by the customer you must work on being objective and open to the customer in a way that allows you to turn perhaps a bad experience for them into a satisfactory one before they leave the range of your voice. Satisfied customers are usually silent and don't usually engage the employee or employer in conversation to compliment the business and their shopping experience. Engage the less than satisfied customer and seek a positive finish.

Being proactive about managing the customer through a positive experience requires listening to the customer and implementing changes that are easy to see from a customer's perspective. Balancing our role as producer and customer is always a consideration, because we need to make sufficient money as producers to be in business tomorrow. Likewise we need to constantly give consideration to the customer to improve their experience with us as producer in every contact. It is the way we generate repeat business and good word-of-mouth publicity. Although we always plan ahead we need to be nimble when what we plan does not occur. Second and third options for action should give us direction when things don't go as planned.

The number of times I have had to consider alternate plans to work my way to an ultimate goal are too numerous to mention. The goals likewise very from personal to business, but the common thread is finding successful alternatives to an original plan that was sound until it met the realities of what goes on in life on a daily basis. The alternatives always need to make room for the customer. If it is a personal goal and you keep falling short consider finding alternatives that fit the objectives of your daily routine. For example if the goal is to loose ten pounds and your objective is to minimize your intake of "junk food" identify alternatives that you like such as fruit, vegetables, or perhaps fiber rich snacks. If they are acceptable substitutes and readily available during those times you normally would eat "junk food" the habit of eating unhealthy food can be managed. If the goal is a business goal such as earning some set value of money per day that turns your cash flow from negative to positive the objective may be to approach twenty potential customers per day to pitch your product or service. An alternative is making appointments with twenty potential customers per day understanding that the customer may need to find time in their schedule for your pitch. If every customer that was considered was discarded because they did not have time for you on your terms your pool of customers would be very small.

Where is the Motivation?

If the customer is busy and needs to schedule an appointment to hear your pitch they are more likely to be able to afford what you are selling. Someone sitting around in their office with too much time on their hands may not be a person that has a positive cash flow themselves. Find your way to the customer one day at a time. Don't make the mistake of thinking if you set up shop the customers will come. You must look for customers and cultivate a relationship that seeks to accommodate customer needs using a plan or alternatives that result in sales. Some of the largest businesses in the world started out small. They did not necessarily start out in poverty, but there are even a few of those examples. You need to focus on doing what you can daily to plan for that positive cash position. Shed negative cash behavior, such as consuming goods and services that are lifestyle choices not choices that contribute to making you fiscally sound.

As this economy bumps along with some good days and some bad days your focus needs to center on those customers that never seem to go away and how you can reach out to them and serve them regardless of the economy. If you doubt the existence of a customer look at the larger picture. The economy in the United States regardless of the significant shocks it has suffered over the last ten years currently still has a gross domestic product of approximately 14 trillion dollars. What are you producing to contribute to that number? What are you buying that contributes to that number? Finally what can you sell that will contribute to that number? The customers are out there even if they are not knocking on your door you should be knocking on their door. Make an effort today that adds something to that GDP, gross domestic product, and join other businesses in their effort to serve a customer that needs better goods and services at a price they can afford.

Partnering with another business is another strategy for one person businesses. You can be their back office where work that only needs to be done occasionally gets done by you. If you have special skills the chance of finding a partner is greater, but even unskilled work has value if a customer thinks the price is right. Businesses larger than yours will always need occasional help during busy times, but they also need help saving money by contracting you on a temporary basis during slow business periods. Do the homework to determine who needs what you provide. Be clear when introducing yourself and what you can do. Give them an easy way to pay you for what you do and explain why they can save money using you over another choice. Be brief and to the point with every potential customer, but be relentless in a search to find that customer that needs what you can provide.

As you discover those first customers that will buy they will energize you and motivate a search for more customers. You will say to yourself, why did I wait so long? If you specialize be the best and be able to show customers a comparison between your work and that of the competition. If you offer multiple products or services try to keep them relative to one another. Although I have come across some of the oddest products in the grocery store, as a small business customers like businesses that have a focus and know how their products compliment one another to serve the customer. Keep it simple in your first efforts to start a one person business. If you sell garden supplies don't make candy bars part of what you offer. When you are focused it helps review technical indicators that keep you on a successful path toward positive cash flow and profitable business long term. Keeping your customer satisfied will be the fuel for your motivation so manage customer satisfaction carefully.

The customers that keep this economy going are an element that you can depend on to provide you with your next job. As an employee or as a small business person, the customer is a constant factor that will always provide an opportunity to become a working part of a thriving community. Customers that buy what we make available in the marketplace on a daily basis are improving economies throughout the world as we recover from the latest recession. Customers have provided work before and they will do it again. We as individuals need to have confidence and prepare for the opportunity that will become available as we seek to serve the customer. Successful people depend on many customers to sustain their wealth, but only a few customers may be necessary to sustain a comfortable way of living for you over the next weeks, months or years. Consider the customer as you search for work.

Where is the Motivation?

How can getting back to work be so simple and still seem so difficult? The opportunity that waits for us as we prepare will not be advertised anywhere it will just be available everywhere we go. If you travel in search of opportunity you may find it in greater abundance. If you stay in your community it will be there, but it will still require your preparation and searching for it none the less than if you had traveled to find it. In today's world you can find opportunity to work and prosper while sitting in your pajamas at home if you only know where to find the customer and provide them with a product or service.

How can unemployment numbers be so high if so much opportunity exists? Many people have lost touch with the customers and are uncomfortable connecting with new customers. Customers can be demanding. They generally expect to get value for money spent. Are you prepared to give a measure of value that is competitive with anyone else in the world? If the answer is yes you can probably work at home in the middle of the night sitting in a comfortable chair. If the answer is no, you may need to travel to a place where opportunity is so abundant that there is enough left over for you. Only you can determine how competitive you are willing to be for the customers that exist.

Through the years I have served a wide range of customers and they never have questioned my being a part of the marketplace. Likewise you can be an active member of any marketplace you choose to be if you first recognize the customer. Customers looking for better value are usually willing to overlook the amenities of your storefront. Whatever you offer will be compared to many more offerings and the customer will decide.

If your first effort is at an open market in the neighborhood that sells you space and facilities to present what you have to offer, the customer will determine how long you can afford to pay for the space. Open market places usually have a ready made level of traffic during the week or on the weekends. Customers may need to see your space in place for more than one weekend before they listen to you pitch what you have to sell.

If you choose instead to look for work as an employee and serve internal customers get to know something about the business

Where is the Motivation?

before you approach them in search of employment. People that run the business are internal customers that create structure and connect the external customer to the services you as an employee provide. It is not always an efficient operation and employees may not benefit beyond a minimum wage. You have the choice between employing yourself or seeking to be employed by others.

Be optimistic about your chances to find customers that fuel the motivation you need to move forward every day. Be efficient in the way you spend your energy. Avoid spending your energy on negative thinking. Look for positive places to spend your energy. You need the customer, but what you provide is what the customer needs.

Chapter 5

Who Can Help?

Look inside yourself first. It is the easiest to do, the most convenient to do, and the place we all need to start. In an effort to be self reliant we must get in the habit of calling on ourselves first for solutions when we stumble. We may need others help ultimately, but the place to start is within ourselves. How many times have I had to call on myself to figure it out? Looking back over a lifetime of 65 years the times are to numerous to count. Some of those times came when I was very young, while others occur as I speak.

My life as a child was not a difficult life as I look at the devastation from natural disasters and poverty around the world. It was a time when like any other child I was more dependant on others to point the way when I would stray from what was acceptable and within the bounds of acceptable behavior. I tended to be a bit more introverted and introspective than others. When I would screw up I usually withdrew into my own world in an attempt to figure it out. At some point If I was overwhelmed I would ask for help with the understanding that I was still part of the solution. One such instance was when I was 16 years old and had a broken down eight year old vehicle. Not knowing where to start I asked the neighbor that had sold me the vehicle, because at the time of the sale he offered to help if I had a problem with the car. He surprised me when he located the technical manual that had served him for eight years and proceeded to teach me everything I needed to know about replacing the worn clutch plate. After making that repair that frankly surprised both of my parents I was confident I could do almost any repair with a little guidance.

As an adult the first recollections I have of either needing to call on myself or ask for help revolved around my work. I happened to work in an industry that was cyclical by nature and when business slowed down the prospect of unemployment became a fact of life. Unemployment was never a time I enjoyed even if I

Who Can Help?

would do what I could to keep up appearances. It always made me feel a bit out of control. It was during these times and through some amount of introspection that I discovered the customer. As a person that tended to look within first I probably overlooked some good advice from relatives and people I knew then that had experience in the business world. Looking within may be the place to start, but it cannot stop there when you are looking for work. It may even be a good idea to move back and forth between self reliant questioning and asking for help from others. Many times while considering how I could align my interests with a customer I had many instances that did not quite connect. It took a second and third look at the dynamics of an unemployment situation to realize how connecting with a customer would end that particular situation.

Each individual brings their own set of conditions to an unemployment situation and that is another compelling reason to look within for some guidance. If you leave what you know best about yourself out of any consideration you may never achieve your goal not to mention your full potential. You also bring a purpose for why you do what you do and only you can know the detail behind your passion for doing one thing instead of another. The guidance you provide for yourself can be what carries you through some of the most difficult times. When help is needed remember you need to contribute to the solution, so the outcome truly reflects you. Secondly, be quick to listen to what other people can contribute. Many solutions are apt to exist, but you need to decide on the steps you will take to insure greater confidence as you move toward full employment.

Align your thinking with fully employed people that have accountability to customers. While unemployed you may not have a big circle of friends that will share their perspective on staying employed. Consider successful business people that are interviewed everyday on business television or even on local news channels. These interviews although not aimed at you and your needs can be helpful if you listen for the persons attention to customer needs and their approach to solving problems that may have threatened their business success.

Who Can Help?

The problem with unemployment is that unless the economy is boiling with activity staying employed can be problem for anyone in the business of serving customers. Recently I needed to have some collision work done and the first bump shop I went to seemed to be quite busy and needless to say their estimate for the work reflected a business that did not need the work. Disappointed but knowing of other very capable smaller shops I continued to the second collision shop. I was surprised to see a very empty shop. A second surprise was the estimate for work it was approximately one third of the first shop. Knowing the owner and the quality of his work I quickly agreed to his price and made arrangements to have the work done. The difference between the first business and the second seemed to be the size not the quality of the work. I asked if the lack of ice and snow was slowing his business and his answer was interesting. Despite his work with many insurance companies it seems the insurance companies have been favoring the large collision shops with multiple locations. Obviously the inflated prices were paying for some redirection of business.

When business is scarce each business has its' own advantage. Larger businesses can offer service over a larger geographic area, whereas small one man businesses can offer the individual not dependent on an insurance company an excellent price. Same quality, better time, better price and personal service wow! As a consumer I just earned a bonus for getting more than one estimate. Plus I gave an old business friend work he needed. We learn everyday more about business when we work to be better consumers. As customers we discover what the customer wants and what they will do to find it.

Help you need is virtually available 24 hours a day 7 days a week and 365 days a year. Although business hours may be more limited than those hours, what you do between the close of business one day and the opening of business the next day will make help available to you when business opens. Doing your homework during those hours after business closes and before they open can make getting the help you need easy. Neglecting your responsibility to be a part of the solution will probably yield unsatisfactory results.

Who Can Help?

Part of what I do when preparing to ask for help is to organize the problem in a way that makes it easy to explain. Sometimes just the act of making clear what the problem is can point you to a solution. Here is a simple example, I needed some wallpaper removed in a short period of time, because I was selling my house and one of the conditions was to remove the wallpaper. Although I had made some progress doing the job myself, I decided to call a more experienced person and get a quote from them. As I took inventory of what needed to be done I recalled that the new owner asked that the walls be made ready to paint. Since the person I selected was a painting contractor that would be bidding on the paint work to be done I was less concerned that his wallpaper removal work would meet the requirements the new owner had established. If he was to be the painter of choice he would need to live with the results of his own work. The painter was a friend of a business associate and came highly recommended. As things worked out the painter chosen to do the wallpaper removal also won the contract for new paint work to be done. The new owners became friends that we visit occasionally and they have expressed their satisfaction with the work done more than once. Organizing access to the house and specifications the work needed to meet within a rather a short period of time helped the painter get the job done on time and to the satisfaction of all parties. As I oversaw the work I was impressed that the painter had all the tools and assistance he needed making me glad I had handed the work off to a professional. The most important pieces that needed to be organized before calling the painter were the schedule, the "paint ready" requirement, and a recommendation from a trusted source. After establishing the schedule it was clear to me that the job was beyond what I could do myself.

An example of help I needed while looking for work likewise came down to organizing my questions ahead of time. I was scheduled to visit a potential customer on a Monday morning after a telephone conversation on Friday. I was aware of the company and generally the types of work they had done, but I was less aware of the people at the company. I spent the weekend reviewing their company at the library in an effort to learn more about the individuals that ran the company and the culture of the

Who Can Help?

company before visiting them for the first time. The homework paid off, because there were a number of people mentioned in the library references that need to be in on final decisions. Without asking questions I already knew where these people were in the organization of the company. When I later met them I mentioned the references and how it was helpful getting acquainted with the company. Although they complained that the some library references had obsolete information they were favorably impressed with my efforts to learn more about the company. I continued to ask more questions about the company and the work they did recently creating some common bonds based on our shared experience in the industry. The day ended well with an open ended contract for work that lasted several months.

When you need help reach out to people that can give you new ideas. Even if the solution is clear but out of reach for you others may have creative ways of accomplishing the same goal. If you don't happen to have friends that are business savvy use the library for current business leaders and their perspective on how new business is getting a foothold in this challenging economy. The economy and business within it is dynamic and ever changing.

Just when we thought we were putting the financial crisis of 2008 behind us we start to hear about a sovereign debt crisis brewing in Greece and Portugal that is threatening euro region countries and their ability to pay their debts. Today the Dow Jones Industrials dropped 268 points. Obviously it will impact more fortunes than those in Greece and Portugal. The rapid movement in the financial markets creates chaos and opportunity. Most things will look the same when I wake up tomorrow morning, but I will explore opportunities that this chaos is creating tonight and consider what I need to do. An unemployed person with assets needs to consider what they need to do to protect themselves and an unemployed person needs to look for opportunities as the news makes itself felt on main street. What is the connection between something as far removed from our daily lives as a debt crisis in Greece and Portugal and the next person you speak to about work? People that are potential customers and potential employers generally have assets and a natural instinct to protect them from

Who Can Help?

loss. A casual conversation they have that informs them of the event and the possible impact might be welcomed information they could use to their advantage. If you were one of the first to bring it to their attention it may improve any opinion they have of you.

Being well informed and able to talk intelligently about news of the day while declining the position of expert can be an asset. It is all part of what you may need to do to connect in a positive way with your customer or employer. Casual discussions with acquaintances can be a way to help you hone an ability to establish a quick connection with customers and employers in interviews. Being outgoing, friendly and well informed are a part of what all employers look for in potential employees. If you have a friend that fits that description try to model their behavior in those situations. Someone can help you by just being a good example.

Help you need beyond your personality and ability to engage in conversation targets your skill or knowledge relative to products and services customers need. You can build a job around a single skill, but you must have expert level either skill or knowledge. Finding help with learning what you need to know can start with the library, but it must quickly move to the business world. The reason I say this is because so many skills are enhanced by the experience of getting the job done. You may be able to find a reference in the library that tells you step by step how to excavate and build a basement for a home, but it may not be how contractors typically do that job. There are always more ways than one to get a job done, but the contractor has used innovative ways to meet building codes and get the job done under adverse conditions and in a short period of time for a price the builder can afford. When computers were new to the individual, many individuals knew more about the equipment than the people selling the equipment. Skill and knowledge are two things you should seek help enhancing, because they are important to customers.

Finding help on the internet requires a fair amount of caution to avoid the scams and routine misinformation that is so wide spread. Look for businesses and organizations that have more than a presence on the internet and have a reputation to protect. If you are looking for skill remember it must at some point be hands on and have a direct connection to an established business if it is to be a credible source of knowledge. If you are simply looking for knowledge consider the accreditations that brick and mortar institutions have as a place to start in your search for knowledge. You wouldn't want to buy the services of an unlicensed doctor anymore than you would want to buy the services of a school without a reputable accreditation. Even credential institutions have their failings and you must be rigorous in your search for the best institution to serve your needs. Make the list of those under consideration shorter by eliminating those that would not get consideration by your customer or employer.

Over the years I have attended many schools and colleges in a search for skill and knowledge that would help either prepare me for a job or customer. The competition or lack of compatibility between institutions sometimes resulted in a loss of credits in transferring from one to another. Accreditation helps eliminate some of that problem. If you already have established sufficient knowledge from institutions and need a more specialized targeted understanding then some of the unaccredited business products offered to the general public may have merit. Make what you purchase limited and targeted so you can evaluate what you buy against the results you expect. There needs to be a direct connection between the understanding you acquire and the job you do everyday. I have used targeted training to boost my income throughout my lifetime and will continue to use it anytime I think I can make a positive difference.

Of all the schooling I have had over the years, the education I have found the most enjoyable and profitable has been targeted training. It is short in length, results are real and meaningful and they can be profound in the way it impacts your life. One of the more recent examples of this in my life has been weight loss. I have had to struggle to control my weight for many years. Although I have had success in the past, it never lasted very long. Now after some rather targeted training I have achieved a loss of some sixty pounds and maintained it without great difficulty for more than one year. Not all attending are successful but many are and have greater achievements to point to. I find it remarkable and enjoy my new life

Who Can Help?

less the sixty pounds. Anyone that struggles with a weight problem would tell you that loosing the weight can impact your life in many ways. Another recent example of targeted training that has made a profound difference in my life has been some money management training. As I approached my retirement it did not look as if I could afford to live comfortably without continuing to work. After that training that I subscribe to on a yearly basis I am glad to report that not only have I retired but three years later despite the chaos in the financial markets retirement is affordable.

If I were younger and unemployed at this time my focus on the help needed would be about the same, because connecting with the customer and having a skill or knowledge to sell is not age sensitive. If you want to be a part of the economy you need to stay engaged in pursuing customers and seeking help along the way as needed. Getting help that makes a difference occurs when you seek help. Sometimes that help is purchased and other times it is offered advice that is generalized and needs to be refined to find the nuggets that help you. However you come by the help you need it is what you do with it when it presents itself. Seek slow progress toward full employment that keeps you engaged while you seek new opportunities that have greater promise. Sitting on the sidelines is not an option for people that want to be available for the customer. As a customer you would not seek out the business owner if they decided to stay home and leave their business closed. It may diminish your opinion of that business, and you are naturally less likely to do business with someone that is not fully engaged in the market.

When I was younger customers rewarded me for what I knew and for my ability to execute a plan that got them what they wanted. Today customers have not changed much. If you need help understanding the customer, reflect on your own experience as a customer. Take responsibility for getting the customer what they want every chance you get. Listen to business leaders that have a record of success. Compare their path to the path you are following. Where have they received help along the way to success? Are they succeeding in this business environment? When are customers rewarding successful businesses that are both small and new? Are there low debt businesses among those that are succeeding? The help most people consider first is financial help, but can you identify a business that you can enter with small startup costs? All businesses are not created equal when it comes to startup costs. Seeking employment as a business requires starting with a business model that can limit startup costs while seeking high cash flow. If the business has higher than normal capital costs for equipment consider renting equipment on a job by job basis. This allows you to draw a reasonable wage from every contract and minimize monthly loan payment for equipment.

Help is not where you begin it is what you look for when obvious solutions to a problem do not work. Some consideration of how you have overcome difficulty in the past needs to be a first consideration even if it is easier to ask someone else to point out a solution. Solutions that you have used in the past are important because they involve you as part of the solution. Handing problems off to someone else to solve is usually expensive and will always require your approval to implement. So if you must approve of something why not start with solutions you have approved of in the past? If the problem is new and unfamiliar find a new application of an old solution. Only you can define what you are willing to do to resolve problems that require big and small effort, so start with familiar solutions that may need new application.

Being young may limit your experience, but that is why getting familiar with how other business people started out and overcame adversity is important. Learn from others life experience as opposed to having to learn everything slowly by trial and error. Solutions more often are a record of history not a part of something that someone is trying to sell you. Quick solutions that are being sold by a attractive advertisement are less likely to resolve a problem than are the lessons successful business people freely reveal in public conversations. Find ways to listen to business leaders that review their years of experience. It is usually free and more helpful than most of what you can buy off the shelf of any store.

Sometimes help is found not while looking for help but while looking for a solution. If you are seeking customers for a product or a service the first customer contact should be helpful as you learn what leads you to more customers. If the marketplace you choose is busy consider the businesses around you that attract customers. What are customers telling you directly about what you have to sell? It can tell you what is right and wrong and where your effort needs to go next. Do not let what the customer has to say go to waste. A customer once told me that they did not have equipment for moving large assemblies from machine to machine. Although, the final piece of equipment they produced was large it needed to be composed of many smaller assemblies that could be carried by hand from machine to machine for final preparation. As the designer I needed to accommodate my customer. My early training was more in tune with large fabricators that had an abundance of lift trucks and cranes, but working within the customers requirements kept me in business.

Does your customer have unique requirements? Sometimes the adjustment may be a minor inconvenience for you, but a must for a larger customer with less flexibility in their schedule. Some of the adjustments you make to accommodate customers make you a preferred vendor. Let the customer guide your development. Even the most innovative products and services are test marketed to get feedback from potential customers. When products or services fail to satisfy customers they are either improved or replaced, if not by the provider then by the competition. Many new products and services look to resolve what customers have long complained about but have not found. How can the customer help you discover the product or service you want to deliver?

Find help while seeking to help customers find what they are looking for on any given day. Some people that need help seek to provide something that does not currently exist and likewise serve the customer. Products and services that are new to the market may not have any demand, because customers do not know they exist. It does not need to be a new electronic device. It can be something as simple as servicing a vehicle, lawnmower or computer at the customers location. Finding ways to make what you sell more convenient to obtain can expand the marketplace.

Who Can Help?

Make finding the help you need a way of serving someone else and avoid the stigma of asking for help. So many times we avoid asking for help. By helping others you remove that stigma. Provide something for someone that cannot afford to pay as an act of charity and except praise as your payment. Find a customer that can afford to pay and collect the first dollar as a small business. Many businesses provide charity as a way to give back to the community that has kept them in business. Establishing a charitable effort does not need to wait 30 years. Despite being unemployed there are ways you can contribute in small ways to your community that give you a opportunity to experiment with new ways to serve customers.

If charity organizations turn you off try helping someone that needs help in a more direct way. Just the act of helping seems to improve our attitude and outlook on life in general. Knowing you can make a difference in someone else's life may be the way to discover you can make a bigger difference in your own life. Anytime I feel a bit down there is nothing that makes me feel better than doing something for someone else. If you need work the first thing you need to address is any lack of activity. Use opportunities to help others as a way to get moving again. Once you are active look for opportunity to sell to others what you may provide as a gift for someone less fortunate.

Paying customers are usually grateful that you have put effort into developing a product or service that truly is needed at a price they can afford. As you look for or review what you have to offer compare it to other similar products and services. Do you provide something that can be distinguished from all the other similar offerings? What niche do you fill with what you have to offer? It is important to know the answer to these questions before the customer asks you.

How can the customer have so much impact over so many aspects of the market and your ability to be a part of the market? The customer is a part of any marketplace transaction. Avoiding consideration of the customer will always put a business in peril. This is not a new consideration, but one that has been in place as long as there have been markets that provide goods and services for

Who Can Help?

customers. Small business and big business alike must consider the customer. The greatest help a business or anyone seeking employment will find comes by way of the customer. The customer informs the business and the employee of the current terms and conditions that expand the growth of business and the prospect of new employment. If you are unemployed can you identify the customer you want to serve? If you are interested in starting a business can you describe the profile of customer that is most likely to help you? If you are in business and sales are lagging who are the new customers you hope to attract?

The help the customer provides may help overcome many shortcomings in either your job search or business model. The customer may not tolerate people that seem to have a low energy level. They may not tolerate a person that is not organized. Customers individually and collectively may reject uncompetitive offers without telling you that you are not competitive. The customer may not allow you to continue sloppy bookkeeping that drains profit from your effort or spend the profit before you earn it. No matter where you start in your effort let the customer help put you on a path that leads to success.

Saying the market is bad and the customer is no longer buying is not where you end, it is where you begin. Customers are always buying something, they may not be buying what you are selling, but they are always buying something. If what you sell is not on the customer's shopping list, let the customer guide you to something that can support the life you want to live. Let the customer give you a new reason to be excited about what you have to offer. As a casual observer you can find many opportunities that customers support today.

The market is what it is and you must learn to engage it and the existing customers to make a difference in your life today. Waiting for better times or customers that see it your way is not an option. Today is the day that customers are ready and willing to show you the way to prosperity. Customers are not usually willing to wait for service. Seek and find customers everyday in an effort to help yourself to what they have to offer in the way of help.

Who Can Help?

When the customer asks for direction it is an instruction as to their interest and the need they are trying to meet. Today I am happy to report another great customer experience. I called a bank that had mishandled several payments on an account over the last several months. Although I was prepared for an argument, I could not thank them enough for the service they provided. They quickly remedied the problem and gave me useful information on how I could avoid future problems. Secondarily, they were able to give me some cost saving information regarding other services they could provide. When customers are treated well they tend to do more business with those businesses that react well to complaints.

Managing customer complaints well is a consideration all businesses large and small need to do well. As a micro business, a business that may only have a fractional employee, customer service can be what helps grow the business into a small business that employs many people and supports a community. The reason is that word of mouth advertising is much more powerful, because it usually comes from a satisfied customer. The customer will usually express their early doubts and how they were overcome by the service they received. Treating an individual customer well touches many people in a single effort.

Today's plan to get help from a customer must include answering any and all complaints that a customer may have. Be prepared to document the complaint, outline opportunities to remedy the complaint and finally document how the complaint was resolved. Customers in a difficult market will expect better treatment when it comes to customer service. In an effort to avoid problems engage the customer and encourage the steps they need to take to remedy any dissatisfaction they may have with a product or service.

The recent problems a foreign automaker has encountered with their product will be a lesson for the world and one that more than one automaker will derive help from for years to come. The customer can be a voice of encouragement or a voice of ridicule. Be quick to give the customers words value and consideration. Help yourself by helping the customer. Do not wait until the customers' words cost you twenty five percent or more of the company value

Who Can Help?

before you heed their message. As a person new to business let the customer guide you to success. Customers are not reluctant to share their emotion when it is strong, either positive or negative.

If you lack a job or a business let the customers you observe show you what they will pay for in the worst of times. Look, listen and learn what the customer will spend their money on. Use many perspectives to view a target customer to get a true picture of the motive behind the purchases any customer makes. Begin to formulate a plan that makes you a part of the market. Answer the question; why would a customer buy from me? If you have a convincing answer you may have new direction and renewed reason to once again serve a customer.

Does the customer demand patience? Does the customer require attention to detail? Will the customer stand before you or will they just be one of many that you will never know personally? Regardless, you must learn the rhythm of their willingness to buy what it is you have to sell and be willing to deliver on their terms. It may require you to acquire new skill or simply more discipline in how you do business from this day forward. Whatever the winning combination is to unlock profit going forward it will require more than a passing interest to establish what really works for you.

Work in the moment. Examining the past has value as does visualizing the future, but nothing satisfies the customer more than your attention the moment they ask for it. Let one good experience serve as stepping stone to the next good experience. Interruptions in your service need to be managed in a way that gives the customer control of the experience. Being available to serve the customer will be rewarding if you learn to anticipate the pattern of success.

Unemployment and under employment is not a unique experience, but you are an individual and that will influence the path you take to make the common experience a place to start and grow. Your ability to meet customer needs and create a place in the world that provides work for you going forward will be tested, but it will be the same test that all businesses face every day. Make the customer your focus every day to insure your success.

Who Can Help?

I have always been comfortable trusting the customer to direct my next move. The customer before you on any given day has considered their needs and is seeking to find a match. If you provide a product or service that is a close match and is competitively priced having the customer before you is a distinct advantage in closing a sale that day. It only takes one customer to start a business, but it takes repeated sales to one or more customers to sustain a business.

Seek help from one customer to start a business and build a relationship while you seek others to follow in their path to your door. Let the preparation and plan you have spent time developing guide your first steps, but let the customer be the guide that secures a business plan that works day to day. Your plan needs to consider every step in any process you have considered, but it needs to be flexible enough to keep any customer engaged along the path to another sale.

If you are seeking to obtain a job you must be willing to negotiate the terms you are willing to work for over time. Like a small business you have a right to refuse any work that does not match your willingness to commit to hours and conditions that you find objectionable. Over the years I have turned away work as an employee and as a business for a wide variety of reasons. Likewise I have been rejected by employers and customers alike for any number of unknown reasons. Identifying new opportunities that give you alternatives when you are either rejected or you reject an offer is the work that you need to do every day. Let the customer stimulate the positive attitude you will need to survive the recessions you will encounter over the years.

Customers by nature will help you determine what you will and will not do either as an employee or as a business. Customers generally seek services and products to meet their needs and wants. Customers are buying something 24 hours a day somewhere in the world. If you seek to work for a customer at any particular time during that day you must consider where the customer can be found and what you are willing to do to satisfy that customer. If you are unemployed and looking to sell an item from a closet or a garage, how do you reach a customer? If you are unemployed and are interested in selling your ability to organize a customer's closet, how do you reach a customer? In today's world several options are available, but they all are based on old tried and tested methods of reaching customers. If you choose to look for a customer on the internet you would probably be more successful by listing your product online and enabling ways for the customer to find you. Customers more often seek a product or service than they advertise to sell either. The same is true of the internet. People did not set up markets to seek products and services, businesses set up markets to allow people to shop for the item or service they sought. Become a part of the marketplace where customers shop.

One reason many people are turned away when they seek employment is because they are sorting through every possible employer instead of marketing to businesses that are actually interested in expanding their workforce. Granted that is a much smaller number but it always is. In the best of times business is not in the business of employing people as much as they are in the business of making a profit and expanding their revenue. Seeking new employees is a function of replacing employees and expanding business. Before you approach a business for consideration as an employee or as an added service, consider how you can contribute to either their top line growth, or their bottom line profit.

Give the customer a reason to think about either hiring you or buying what you have to sell. If a business has just suffered a recent decrease in business they will be buying products and services that quickly slow their losses. Businesses that are in a slow but steady decline are more inclined to buy something that will improve their growth over time, because they have probably made cost saving changes during their decline. Although cost savings are still attractive growing their revenues will be motivating their purchases. Let the story you tell others about your success include the way you were able to help customers make money and save money allowing them to do more of what they would do with the extra resources.

Seek the customers you are most likely to help based on the specific product or service you have to offer. Avoid all random customer encounters.

Who Can Help?

Sift and sort through all of the best customers until you identify several customers that have the means and motivation to purchase what you have to sell. Consider how the customer will benefit and how quickly they will improve their revenue or profit from their purchase. Consider the promotions that might interest the customer and the place you will engage the customer in an effort to make a sale. Let these technical indicators focus your energy on customers with the greatest potential.

Only you can prepare to approach customers with what you have to sell. If you are convinced that you have what the customer wants, share a positive message that connects with the customer in the first encounter. Engage each customer in a way that leaves them wanting to do business with you. Making a pitch to new customers that can help you is part science and part art. The percentages vary with every individual, but start with 80 percent science and 20 percent art. The science must consider all of that less than interesting information that gives your product or service value in the market when compared to competing products and services. The art of the sale will improve the perception of your product or service in support of the science. Most people do a fine job of assembling the science, but they loose some benefit of the science by doing a poor job on the art that presents the science to each and every customer.

Considering your product presentation from the customers' point of view is one way to find the flaws. The benefits to the customer from the producers' perspective are always more generous than that of the actual customer. Take a sample of your product and offer it in a limited way to actual customers and do it in a way that encourages their feedback that will allow you to adjust your product for a wider audience. The customer is usually not timid when it comes to brief first impressions. Test marketing is done by companies small and large alike. Taking what you have to sell to market also lets you get a feel for all of the many things you can only second guess on your desk at home. The market is dynamic and will impact your product or service sales differently from one day to another.

Who Can Help?

When I think back on those early days when I offered to do design on a contract basis virtually every customer wanted to get a limited sample of the work before they would commit to more extensive contracts. It always put the customer in control of the volume of product or service they would be committed to, giving them an easy way to expand their capacity for work yet manage the cost of services over time. Today businesses are likewise restrained in what they buy. If you can give another business the advantage of expanding the service they provide without incurring long term commitments to labor or capital they will be willing to consider your proposal. The next step is making what you contribute look like a normal part of the business you serve. Contracted services are usually back office services that are not in direct contact with the businesses customers. Another popular model is the consolidated marketplace.

There are some great examples of common markets today. Some large retailers have within their walls smaller businesses that simply maintain a counter during normal business hours. Web sites likewise are a composite of many producers that may all be independent except that they all receive customer orders from a single website that processes the orders. Just like a shopping mall there are many examples on a large and small scale that imitate the shopping mall model. Finding your niche within a market that encourages collaboration on elements that drive traffic for all businesses is another way of sharing the cost of marketing and facility management. Even if you are just starting a micro business there are ways to become part of a market at a reasonable cost. Weekend markets and single events organized around holidays provide some of the best opportunities. If you are struggling at a fixed address find ways to reach out to customers over the web and by telephone.

Even though the customer does not organize or manage the various marketplaces that exist consider the customer when you pick a marketplace. The organizers of marketplaces want businesses that both pay their rent and enhance the shopping experience for the customer. To avoid buying worthless space you must consider the profile of the shopper that frequents the market. Are the customers that are a part of the existing traffic likely to associate what you sell with the marketplace you are considering? An office space in a medical complex would not be the place I would expect to find fishing lures. However an open air market with a diversity of products might be just the place to offer fishing lures. There are those exceptions that make you wonder if customers will buy just about anything in some of the most unlikely places. Every spring grocery stores add lawn furniture among the grocery aisles. Summer brings bathing suits and beach balls to the same aisles. Fall always makes room for Halloween costumes and lawn ornaments. Finally the end of the year demands blow up lawn decorations and television equipment. I cannot say with any assurance that these product rotations are profitable, but grocery stores with these odd selections have done this for several years and likely do profit. The grocery stores are creating a marketplace for these odd choices and hope to capture some spontaneous purchases among the groceries rather than picking a market. It is similar to you having a much wider selection of products in a catalog that may work against the theme of the majority of products you offer. A new business needs to focus on fewer products and services in an effort to serve the customer well.

Describe the customer you hope to serve. What is the profile of a customer that will regularly buy what you have to sell? What kinds of businesses do your customers already frequent? Can you locate your product or service in the market that already serves your customer? If you have an existing business that is not getting the advantage of foot traffic that helps build your business you need to market what you sell in more ways than one. Virtual locations and temporary locations help make more customers familiar with your brand. These same methods are effective for new businesses that have no location in a permanent marketplace. Finding effective ways to inform customers require creativity if you are to do it at a reasonable cost. Both established businesses and new businesses must test market ways to reach customers. I am not talking about one or two tests, many tests throughout the year to identify what works and when it works best. It may seem at times like marketing is a second only to the work you do producing the product or your service of choice.

Who Can Help?

I think it should be clear that if you expect a customer to help you stay in business or support the work you do as an employee you have an obligation to give the customer your attention. The best stories of business succeeding are those reported on by satisfied customers. Any example of how a business has pleased a customer can be used to guide your effort to serve a customer today. Examples from 40 years ago can be as relevant as those today. New technology adds opportunity to replaces lost opportunity. The best examples are of the opportunities created for business by the introduction of computers, because they are so numerous the lost opportunities are looked at as obsolete in many cases.

Business succeeded when it found a way to enable an entire office to do what perhaps only one or two people could do efficiently. Consider the ability of a person to sort through information before the computer existed. After the computer and some of the early database products the same person was not only able to sort through much more information, but so was the entire office. The computer made reliance on any one person obsolete. Today cellular telephones are another innovation that is quickly adding capability and mobility to business people worldwide. People are finding ways to be productive and mobile at the same time without any particular business telling them what to do. You as an individual have at this time a level of technology available that expands the possibilities while we live through one of the most debilitating recessions in many years.

To get through this period and be prosperous you as an individual will need to make sense of the paradox of increased opportunity on one hand and increased unemployment on the other. Perhaps it is not a paradox at all but instead a paradigm shift that is occurring. In other words the increased opportunity and high unemployment are not opposing forces but instead working hand in hand to transition to a more productive model of work that we may not fully comprehend. Another possibility is that the business model and business cycle are still intact and we are just feeling the impact of an out of balance condition that is still out of balance. Finally we may have percentages of each of those conditions at work. All things considered the last scenario is probably the most likely. How does knowing that help us get back to work? Let's start with the customer. If the customer is the way to remedy either an unemployed status or slow business environment then we need to understand what the customer is buying that keep the majority of people employed. It is important to remember that most people are employed regardless of the despair that is expressed by the chronically unemployed or the business failures that persist.

The motivation behind many of the purchases that support eighty percent or more of the population varies on a scale of needs and wants. Customers may not reveal their motivation by the purchases they make over time, but they do make clear what is worth their money. Retail sales are up in the first month of 2010 when compared to December of 2009. This is a bit less than three percent split between gasoline, electronic/appliance stores with about a one percent increase in restaurant sales. These sales are still down when compared to the first month of 2008. Furthermore the gross domestic product for 2009 was well over 14 trillion dollars (http://www.bea.gov/newsreleases/national/gdp/2010/txt/gdp4q09_2nd.txt). This means that although sales have dropped over the last year there is still an enormous amount of money being spent in many ways. The improved sales only identify the area that are benefiting on a monthly basis. What we gain from this is confidence that there is a great deal of business being done even during what is by any measure a severe recession.

In an effort to move from where you are today to a more productive and self sufficient tomorrow let the customer guide what you need to do to secure either employment or customers to support your own business. The existence of a 14 trillion dollar economy means that there are opportunities for you to produce and prosper today and everyday going forward.